W0018208

SAGE was founded in 1965 by Sara Miller McCune to support the dissemination of usable knowledge by publishing innovative and high-quality research and teaching content. Today, we publish over 900 journals, including those of more than 400 learned societies, more than 800 new books per year, and a growing range of library products including archives, data, case studies, reports, and video. SAGE remains majority-owned by our founder, and after Sara's lifetime will become owned by a charitable trust that secures our continued independence.

Los Angeles | London | New Delhi | Singapore | Washington DC | Melbourne

ADVANCE PRAISE

What is the role of a madrasa? Should it concentrate on imparting Islamic instruction only and memorizing the Quran in Arabic without understanding the meaning or imbibing the values enshrined? Or should it produce a complete *aalim* (scholar) ready to take his place in the changing world with knowledge of modern science and technology?

The answer to this question is provided by Ziya Us Salam and M. Aslam Parvaiz in *Madrasas in the Age of Islamophobia*.

The book addresses two key questions: How madrasas are falsely accused by some politicians of producing radicalized students who pick up arms and indulge in militancy. And, how some madrasas are trying to find ways to stay relevant in contemporary times by imparting modern knowledge alongside Islamic teachings. The book shall remain relevant for those seeking to reform madrasa education.

Swami Agnivesh, *Former Minister of Education, Haryana; social reformer activist*

Ziya Us Salam and M. Aslam Parvaiz have jointly ventured into the territory that many would consider contested. But the authors have historical facts to back them in their lucid presentation.

The book delves into the history of evolution of madrasas in medieval times in India and elsewhere in the Islamic world. Extending patronage was considered a pious act as learning was valued, which in return earned rulers' legitimacy. Many madrasas emerged as centres of scholarly exchange and medium of carrying forward certain schools of thought. The Madrasa-i-Rahimiyah in

Delhi and Darul Uloom in Deoband, Saharanpur, Uttar Pradesh, are examples of these acting as centres of learning as well as upholders of certain worldview. Maulana Azad had established the Madrasa-i-Islamia in Ranchi with help from many non-Muslims as the largest donor for its establishment was one Rai Saheb Thakor Das, a prominent personality of Ranchi.

In the late 20th century and early 21st century, these institutions were subjected to undue scrutiny for acting as hubs of extremism. Scholars failed to point out inadequacies of their antiquated syllabus and curriculum. Graduates of these institutions have not been abreast with the contemporary realities in the world of knowledge. Instead of removing baggage of backwardness, they are politically targeted and poor man's learning spaces are seen with coloured vision.

The book is the outcome of serious scholarship as it illuminates dark corners of our understanding about madrasas.

Rizwan Qaiser, *Professor, Department of History and Culture, Jamia Millia Islamia, New Delhi*

Lack of familiarity breeds contempt. In the age of the short-cut and of simplistic connections, many of us do not even realize how ill-informed we are about traditions and institutions in the multiverse that is India. This book is an essential reading for all citizens, addressing as it does the richness of an alternative system of education. Madrasas vary as much as do government schools, in terms of facilities and rigour of courses. Perceived as essentially religious seminaries, their strengths—such as the grounding in logic and their multi-language richness—are forgotten. These chapters are timely—covering madrasas of different vintage in different regions of India and of different branches of Islam, their intellectual achievements, and their principled stands on political issues and on matters where Islamic law is at odds with the civil law. The chapters are not all feel-good, soaked in nostalgia. On the one hand, they point out the shortcomings of madrasas, their often outdated syllabus and method of teaching; on the other, they expose as hollow claims of madrasas being the nurseries of terrorism. The book is a must-read.

Narayani Gupta, noted historian and author

The book touches a very important topic that the Muslim community is facing in India rather than all over the world. It would be appreciated by all sections of the society. Some very important and sensitive issues related to madrasas have been dealt with: their infrastructure, contents/syllabus, methods of teaching, resources, management, etc. As far as madrasa syllabus is concerned, surely it is in immense need for updating. The need of the hour is to study both old and new *tafsirs*.

The authors have taken up the issue of terrorism levelled against the madrasas and proved their point in a well-documented way. They advocate reform of madrasa system and their syllabi in the light of modern-day requirements. The language is simple, lucid and attractive. The authors deserve all appreciation.

Ubaidur Rahman, *Associate Professor, Centre of Arabic and African Studies, Jawaharlal Nehru University, Delhi*

MADRASAS
in the **AGE** *of*
ISLAMOPHOBIA

MADRASAS
in the **AGE** *of*
ISLAMOPHOBIA

ZIYA US SALAM

M. ASLAM PARVAIZ

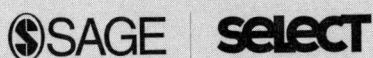

Los Angeles | London | New Delhi
Singapore | Washington DC | Melbourne

First published in 2020 by

SAGE Publications India Pvt Ltd
B1/I-1 Mohan Cooperative Industrial Area
Mathura Road, New Delhi 110 044, India
www.sagepub.in

SAGE Publications Inc
2455 Teller Road
Thousand Oaks, California 91320, USA

SAGE Publications Ltd
1 Oliver's Yard, 55 City Road
London EC1Y 1SP, United Kingdom

SAGE Publications Asia-Pacific Pte Ltd
18 Cross Street #10-10/11/12
China Square Central
Singapore 048423

Published by Vivek Mehra for SAGE Publications India Pvt Ltd. Typeset in 9.5/13.5 pts ITC Stone Serif by Fidus Design Pvt. Ltd, Chandigarh.

Library of Congress Control Number: 2019953962

ISBN: 978-93-5328-929-4 (PB)

SAGE Team: Namarita Kathait, Sandhya Gola and Kanika Mathur

Ammi and Miyan Huzur,
my first teachers in the school of life.

ZIYA US SALAM

My wife Shaheen, all my research and
awareness missions would not have been
possible without her.

M. ASLAM PARVAIZ

Thank you for choosing a SAGE product!
If you have any comment, observation or feedback,
I would like to personally hear from you.

Please write to me at **contactceo@sagepub.in**

Vivek Mehra, Managing Director and CEO, SAGE India.

CONTENTS

PREFACE

Every town worth its name in the Hindi heartland of India has at least one 'Bombay Hairdresser', a delightful euphemism for an elementary barber shop offering 'Bombay haircut' and 's(h)ave'. Nobody has ever asked, 'What is Bombay haircut?' or whether there is one. The little shops with three chairs and a large mirror do brisk business. Of course, loud Hindi film music plays as a value addition. The monotony of tired, shaggy men swatting away flies with an old Hindi newspaper is broken when a little boy enters the premises holding on to the hand of his father. 'The boy needs a haircut', announces the proud father. Promptly, a wooden slab emerges. It is soon put across the armrests of one of the chairs. The youngster sits there, and a 'Bombay haircut' starts. It was probably the same with his father when he needed a haircut as a kid in Uttar Pradesh, Delhi, Rajasthan or Bihar. For generations, sleepy towns of India have revelled in 'Bombay Hairdresser(s)'.

It is much like the ubiquitous 'Prince Tailors' who 'specialize in ladies', gents' and children's dresses'. Every town would have had at least one 'Prince Tailor' offering to stitch 'salwar suit, dress, pant or shirt in 24 hours'. The business was steady until a few years ago when ladies and gents started preferring readymade garments. Many 'Prince Tailors' have since been reduced to penury; some have had their shops shrinking with declining business. Clearly, these are not easy times to be a tailor, 'Prince' or otherwise.

It is much like the madrasas in these parts of the country. Like the tailor and the hairdresser, every township worth its alluvial or sandy soil has had at least one Makkah Masjid, Madina Masjid, or even Bilal Masjid. The names, in a clear throwback to Islamic history, have been glorious; the first two alluding to two of the holiest sites in Islam, the last one to the man who gave the first *azaan*, the prayer call. Not so glorious or edifying is the fate of the men who sit at the gates of these mosques every day, particularly, after Asar, the middle prayer, or on Fridays. These gentlemen, often with luxuriant white beards, a red checked scarf to go with their kurta and pyjamas ending at least an inch above the ankles, are the first to get up at the conclusion of a prayer. Invariably, they represent a madrasa (Islamic seminary) in the vicinity or, more likely, one separated by 50–100 km. 'The madrasa is in a bad shape. The ceiling is leaking, making it difficult for the devotees to offer prayer. Whosoever makes Allah's house here, Allah makes a house for him in Jannah (Paradise),' they announce, asking the faithful to dip into their pockets to help out. Occasionally, they say, 'The madrasa has no money to provide its students with blankets or quilts in winters. It does not have enough money to feed its 60 students. It needs urgent help.' With such words, the madrasa fundraisers quit the prayer congregation and spread a sheet of cloth, or even their scarf, to sit at the entrance of the mosque. This time they back up their spoken words with a few faded photographs of the madrasa to win over the confidence of the people that their money is going to a deserving place. Some of the worshippers give them ₹10 or ₹20, most nothing. Occasionally, a man takes out his wallet to give ₹100. His name is promptly written in the receipt book readily available with the man, and a receipt is provided. Like with the hairdresser and the tailor, it has been that way for generations in towns, and even cities of India. Like the tailor and the hairdresser, the madrasas—the cradle of Islamic learning—are going through rough and challenging times. The funds are low, almost entirely dependent on acts of charity of the believers, or what is euphemistically called community funding. Worse though is the inability of the madrasa management to move with the times. While hundreds of madrasas run without registration, even those with proper documentation and enviable history seem to be at the crossroads, for instance, Madrasatal Uloom in Muzaffarnagar. Blessed with a multi-storeyed building which has 40 rooms for students to stay besides multiple classrooms and a biggish lawn, the madrasa should ideally be extending the best of facilities to its students. Far from it, the students are expected to sleep on the floor, come winter or summer. In summers, when some 40 students sit crouched over the sacred book, two fans with twin blades are supposed to be sufficient to keep them cool. Forget air-conditioned classrooms, even air coolers or sufficient fans are not there. In winters, the students are asked to stir-clean a well-worn-out rug and spread it across the room. At night, the boys lie down, one after the other, on the same rug. There is no sense of private space. Some have a blanket or a quilt to call their own. They are the privileged ones—most are not, as a majority of madrasa students hail from financially poor families, many are first-generation learners. It is for such students that the fundraisers ask for help at the conclusion of prayers at a Madina Masjid or a Bilal Masjid. As for food, it is usually just *dal–chawal* (lentils–rice). Occasionally, when some good Samaritan visits the place, meat is provided. On such days, the management committee members have an elaborate feast: korma, nahari, stew, biryani and kheer. The students are the last to be fed, recipients of what is left at the base of a pressure cooker or *karhai*. It still calls for a celebration! The students accept it all gleefully, letting out a whistle here, or organizing an impromptu game of cricket or football there. Interestingly, in the cricket game, the only thing close to the original is the bat which is somehow procured by one of the guys. The wickets are usually three white lines drawn on a wall, or a tree trunk. No gloves, no pads, no helmets, and it is not a leather cricket ball they play with but a tennis ball. Dressed in loose kurta–pyjamas and swinging wildly at the incoming ball, they present a unique sight.

This is their only picnic. Else, the word has not entered the vocab-ulary of our madrasas. For instance, take a look at the madrasa adjacent to Insan School in Kishanganj. The school is renowned for its educational standards in an otherwise educationally and economically backward district. It has history on its mantelpiece. Although it has seen better days, it hosts an international litera-ture festival. The students of the school, in smart trousers, a shirt and a tie, attend many of the deliberations. The students of the madrasa remain conspicuous by their absence. All through the festival, they remain inside their room at the far end of the sports field, spread across the cement floors of their room in early winters, emerging only to offer prayers at their appointed time. The madrasa does not extend much more than basic facilities in accommodation. It trains them not to understand the chats in English during the festival. It tells them not about the currents of Indian polity, economy and the society. They are like frogs in the well: read, learn, memorize and repeat. From early morning to lunch, then again after a lunch break to the time of middle prayers, the students sit hunched over religious texts. There are no tables, no chairs, just benches to place their books and rough, jute rugs to sit on. Most try to read the Quran in the Arabic original. Some try to memorize it. Only a few senior ones get to read some authentic Hadith from Bukhari or Sahi Muslim. It has been that way, not for decades but centuries, not just here but also at countless madrasas across the country. Incidentally, there is no count of the number of madrasas either. The official figures have wavered from 200 to 6,000! That is for those which are recognized. Add to these a number of unrecognized, informal madrasas giving free education to the poor, and you get a mind-boggling picture of an institution about whose numbers nobody is sure, yet an institution that is at least churning out literate people in a country where every third person is still unable to read and write.

The syllabus of most madrasas in 2019 or 2020 could be replaced with the syllabus of a madrasa in 1920, or even 1870. There is a timelessness to the whole affair which defies the message of the Quran. The book asks the mankind to think, explore and introspect. The madrasas ask the students to concentrate on memorizing the Quran and ask no questions. Any attempt to ask questions is met with a rebuke; a pupil is supposed to toe the line. Education is an evolutionary process. Blackboards are going out of fashion. But in madrasas, time stands still. They make no attempt to provide the students with the latest tafsir, or commentary of the Quran. Many still consult 14th-century work of Ibn Kathir. For them, the works of Abul A'la Maududi, Dr Israr Ahmed and Wahiduddin Khan merit no space. In the timeless world of

Indian madrasas—of course with honourable exceptions in large parts of South India, particularly Kerala—the students are supposed to read and memorize the Quran with a finger on the book, a cap on the head, little inside; it is not unusual to find a hafiz-e-Quran who does not know the meaning of a single surah of the Quran. The students are not given any opportunity to use computers to know the latest in the world of Islam. They are seldom taught secular subjects such as mathematics, English, Hindi and science, or at least provided with the required time and space. This goes against the drive for unification of knowledge so forcefully sought through the Quran and Hadith, and practised for centuries after Prophet Muhammad departed from this world. Till the 12th century, Muslims were in the forefront of scientific scholarship, discoveries and inventions. In this era, many of the greatest philosophers, mathematicians, doctors and historians were Muslims. An important contribution of these early Muslim scholars was the experimental method, which is integral to modern science.

The great interest in knowledge and research that emerged with the rise of Islam is a very significant phenomenon. This thirst for knowledge among the early Muslims was produced by the Quran and by the encouragement given to knowledge by Prophet Muhammad. Practising the teachings of the Quran, these Muslims became experts in many sciences and made significant advances in them, which was a major reason for the widespread Muslim influence that prevailed at this time over a large part of the world. A very important aspect of the passion for knowledge among early Muslims was their holistic understanding of knowledge.

Many of the top Muslim scientists of this time were not just experts in one or the other natural science but also in the religious sciences. For instance, before the noted scientist Jabir ibn Hayyan (721–815) began scientific research, he had stayed in Medina and received knowledge of Islam from Imam Jafar al-Sadiq, a descendant of the Prophet who was a great Islamic scholar. Along the same lines, Zakariya al-Razi and Abu Ali Sina were top medical doctors of their times and well-versed in the religious sciences and philosophy too. In a study of key scientists from the 7th to the 15th century, Charles Gillespie made a list of 132 people, of whom 105 were from the Muslim world. It changed drastically, thanks to an education system that promotes division, not unification of knowledge.

That was then. Today, a student who would have spent about four years in memorizing the Quran would not understand its contents, and often a student would have spent nine years in madrasa without knowing the basics of biological or physical sciences. It has been going on for almost 300 years. The students memorize the Quran without understanding a verse of it. Every year, at the graduation ceremony, usually held 15 days before the onset of Ramadan, the students are given their certificates. On the occasion, they are expected to recite a few verses from the Quran. Most do it dutifully, even gleefully, without knowing the meaning of what they would have recited. The madrasas make them hafiz—one who has memorized the Quran—but prepare them not for a job. With no knowledge of maths, science, English, etc., the best that the students can hope to do is to pick up a job as an imam in some masjid in their village. Or be a muezzin, the caretaker of the mosque. The usual secular jobs are out of their reach. In today's age, they do not know how to send an email. Their only exposure to technology in the big, wide world outside is through a mobile phone, which one of the more fortunate students would have had in the madrasa. The student's personal mobile phone becomes a public phone with each student taking turns to watch a little video, listen to a song or even receive their parents' call! Far from being the moral leaders of the world, the youngsters find the world speaks the language they do not quite understand. With most madrasas not able or willing to lay stress on English learning, it is a vicious circle for students. The madrasas where they spend prime years of their life do not prepare them for this world, concentrating as they are on *akhirat* or the Hereafter. The world around throws up questions for which they are not prepared. The educated Muslims (those who attain education at public schools and universities) outside want them to guide the community on issues such as instant triple talaq and rights of inheritance, even zakaat in the light of the Quran. The secular world expects them to know about the latest in Microsoft or Adobe. The madrasas prepare them for neither. They work in a social and historical vacuum. Far from taking inspiration from the history of Islam and Islamic scholars' achievement, they remain oblivious of faith. The world has marched on from 632 AD, and from the 12th century. The madrasas are stuck there. Forgetting the Quran, they concentrate on *fiqh* (jurisprudence), and are caught in a cul-de-sac.

The madrasas are a world much removed from the 21st century India; it is a world where students are not allowed to wear jeans–T-shirts, watch television or learn secular subjects for fear of going astray. This is from a community which was once ahead of the global fraternity in matters of science and mathematics, a community which gave the earliest astronomers, medical practitioners and mathematicians. It is a community negating its past. It is a community caught in a time warp. The madrasas at the crossroads are symptomatic of what's wrong with the world of believers. A community which made landmark contribution to science has now become tied down to blind imitation and hidebound traditionalism, a community that has now begun considering memorization of certain religious texts as knowledge and penning commentaries on the commentaries of these texts and books on minor aspects of jurisprudence as intellectual work.

All these thoughts found a physical expression in Ramadan 2019. It is a month particularly notable for umpteen number of madrasa representatives visiting mosques to beseech the community to bail them out of the hard times. In the summer of 2019, one representative, sitting at a mosque in Faridabad, claimed to be from the only madrasa in Rudrapur, an area dominated by Sikhs. Another recalled how there was no mosque or madrasa for a community of 10,000 in Haryana. Some were straightforward in their appeal: 'We teach the poor. Please finance the education of a poor child for a year. The reward will continue forever.' Not a single representative of a madrasa talked in terms of opening a science laboratory or adding a library! Every madrasa seemed to face an existential crisis. Around the same time, we stumbled upon Madrasa Rashidia in New Delhi where almost 50 students seek education. The madrasa shares its space with a masjid. It so happened that once volunteers of Khidmat Foundation came to the mosque for their deliberations and discovered the shabby conditions in which the youngsters live. Far from understanding the Quran, they were, unsurprisingly, into rote learning. Knowledge of English, maths, etc., was totally absent. They had no source of entertainment. The only change from a 24×7 indoor life was a visit to a cemetery nearby followed by an aimless walk around a park close to the cemetery. Khidmat Foundation decided to change it and started weekend classes of elementary English, maths and science. After initial opposition from the madrasa management, they succeeded in imparting basic lessons. While in itself it was laudable, it set us thinking: Is this the community that is asked by the Quran to seek knowledge? Why have the believers and their institutions forgotten the basic purpose? Why do they reduce Islam to a set of rituals? And to think, these bricks-and-mortar structures educating the poorest of the poor are accused of being harbourers of terror by opportunist politicians! A more irresponsible charge was seldom made. It set our mind thinking: Are madrasas, which beg for funds to provide two meals to their students, dens of terror or cradles of ignorance? What ails them: Is it lack of funds or their own closed minds or simply a reduction of religion to a set of rituals? *Madrasas in the Age of Islamophobia* is an attempt to peek into the world of Indian madrasas and see how far the community has to travel to revive its days of glory. It is an attempt to go back in time, from the earliest knowledge centres of West Asia to madrasas in medieval India, and finally to post-Independence India, when to be an aalim of Islam from a local madrasa is often synonymous with being ignorant of the world.

ACKNOWLEDGEMENTS

Madrasas in the Age of Islamophobia would not have been possible without the silent but steadfast support of our respective spouses, Uzma Ausaf and Shaheen. Nor can we afford to forget our respective family members or the colleagues and friends at the *Hindu* and *Frontline*, particularly Venkitesh Ramakrishnan, V. Venkatesan, Purnima Tripathi and Anando Bhakto. A note of thanks is due to brother Irfan Ahmed for happily sharing with us details of some of the lesser known madrasas, to Dr S. M. Tariq Nadwi for helping with the research, and to Dr Yoginder Sikand and Ms Nigar Ataulla, who motivated us to write what one has been speaking about in social media. Their support is duly acknowledged. Thanks are due to Professor Aleem Ashraf Jaisi and Professor M. Fahim Akhtar Nadvi for facilitating interaction with madrasas, and to Ms Sunita Reddy for prompt and excellent computing support for some of the write-ups. Also, we would like to express gratitude to Imam Muhibullah Nadwi, Imam Mohammed Salim and brothers V. M. Ibraheem, Savad Rahman, Mohammed Ali, Aslam Khan, Aftab Alam, Rashid Ali, Junaid Ali Syed, Tahir Naqvi and Syed Hassan Kazim for the contribution. Then there were the long-distance prayers of brothers Tausief and Tauqueer Ausaf. Not to forget prompt and selfless help from brothers Khaliquz Zaman and Arshad Sheikh of Jamaat-e-Islami Hind and Mohammed Anwer Hussain of Jamiat Ulama-i-Hind, as also noted scholar of moderate Islam Faizur Rahman sahab. We will be guilty if we don't acknowledge the large-heartedness shown by Noorul Huda, Humera Hayat and Nikhat baji, besides sisters Muslima and Sajida, and brother Aamir Abdur Rashid. Of course, brother Khadim Hussain continues to guide, encourage and anchor, like none other. We are grateful. This book belongs as much to all of them as to the authors.

My Lord, increase me in knowledge

—VERSE 114, SURAH TAHA, THE QURAN

Chapter 1

MADRASAS UNDER A CLOUD

Muhibullah Nadwi
Darul Uloom, Nadwa, Lucknow

'We 100 per cent believe no madrasa student can even imagine taking the life of an innocent person. All the allegations about madrasa students taking to terrorism or the madrasas teaching about terrorism stem from absolute ignorance. Those commenting on the madrasas these days know nothing about them. Most would never have entered a madrasa. Mostly, their opinion is based on the media reports. The media, in turn, hardly knows anything about the working, the academic rigour of life in the madrasa. Yet it insists on writing about the madrasas. It is like writing about an accident without visiting the spot. The madrasas teach about the *ilm* of the Prophet. It is wrong to allege that the madrasas ask the students to wage jihad against the state or society. People who talk of jihad do not even know its true meaning, which is to fight with one's own *nafs*, or control one's desires. Allah did not ask any of the prophets to overthrow established regimes. No prophet ever sought political leadership. They preached about doing good deeds to avoid going to Hell. The madrasas do not teach to overthrow any government or to change the system, but they teach the students that when they leave the madrasa, they must help the humanity establish its connection with the almighty. Their syllabus is independent of political leadership or the prevalent system. The students who pass out of a madrasa denounce homosexuality, vulgarity, illicit relations, alcoholism. They criticize illicit relations between boys and girls. But then there are people who are prone to doing these things. When their personal desires run contrary to such pious teachings, they call madrasa students terrorists. The reality is that they do not have a moral counter to such a narrative of madrasa students.'

'Whether it is the BJP or the RSS making these allegations, they have a misunderstanding about the madrasas. Whatever they know about the madrasas is through the media or propaganda. If, instead, they had relied on finding out the truth, they would have discovered that what the madrasas teach is similar to what their faith preaches too. For instance, in the scriptures of Hinduism, women are advised against interacting with men freely; they are expected to cover themselves in public. They too preach about the worship of one almighty.'

Imam Muhibullah Nadwi explains the meaning of Quranic verses at New Delhi Jama Masjid

As a man who spent seven years in the illustrious Darul Uloom Nadwatul Ulama, and a few more in other small madrasas, Muhibullah Nadwi is as well placed to talk of the madrasa as the best scholars of Islam. 'I am 43 and have spent 20 years in masjid, and another more than 10 years in madrasas,' he says. He has been there, stayed there, interacted with the best, and observed the changes and the challenges. Indeed, he was always destined to be at a madrasa. When little Muhibullah was taking his first steps in life, his parents decided to enrol him in an English medium school, believing the road to prosperity and peace, not necessarily synonymous, was paved through English medium education. Hailing from a small township of Swar in Uttar Pradesh, Muhibullah stayed on to complete fourth standard from a primary school near his place. His heart though was set on studying at a madrasa.

'In my school which was an old school, having been built in 1942, we used to have a prayer, "Lab pe aati hai dua banke tamanna meri". That prayer set me thinking that I must do something for the entire humanity. I sought religious education. The parents did not stop me. My elder brothers were studying in a madrasa though it was not out of choice. I was the only one in the family to go to a madrasa out of choice. Rest all went by compulsion. First, I went to Madrasa Furqania in Rampur. I stayed in boarding and memorized the Quran in two and a half years. The madrasa was good. It provided only basic amenities, like fans and charpoys or takht (wooden cot) to sleep on. We were expected to look after our other needs, like rugs or sheets. There were no coolers those days. Life was simple. Desires were not many.'

Muhibullah memorized the Quran at this madrasa in two and a half years which was spectacular by the prevalent standards as most students take up to four years.

'After *hifz*, I went to a madrasa, Madeenatul Anjuman Muhavirul Islam in Sambhal where I studied for a little over a year. Then I went directly to Lucknow and joined Nadwa. I had attained elementary knowledge of Arabic in Sambhal, but Nadwa was a different world altogether. I had also grown up a little by then, and my life's canvas changed after arriving at such a prestigious institution. I was not nervous. I felt happy. I studied Arabic grammar here, then focussed more on the language. The fiqh classes overall were a mix of Arabic and Urdu languages. At that time, no thought was spared about organ transplant, blood transfusion, etc. These are new concepts. The students were not taught any of those things, though things are changing now. I spent seven years in Nadwa. I became an alim. The madrasa did not help in placement. Their idea has always been that their students should spread the word of Allah. They expect their students to spread the basic things about Islam in the larger society, the concepts of tauhid, the reason and process of creation of humanity, etc. Nadwa expects the students to follow the ways of the prophets, live a life of discipline and self-denial, stay hungry, and desist from worldly attainments; the way the prophets were helped by God, they too will surely get divine help. Instead of coming up with thousands of well-established, well-earning students, it is better, Nadwa believes, if we can produce even a handful of true scholars of Islam. I kind of went astray and ended up in a mosque, though my institution did not object, because a mosque is, after all, an integral part of Islam. Mostly, they prefer their students to live a low-profile life, working for the cause of deen (faith). Tell me, is there any remotely related to terrorism or misconceived ideas of jihad in all this?'

Muhibullah today is the chief imam at New Delhi's Jama Masjid opposite Parliament House. Among the men who have stood in prayer behind him have been the likes of late President Dr A. P. J. Abdul Kalam, former Vice President Hamid Ansari, stalwarts of the Congress, Bharatiya Janata Party, Rashtriya Janata Dal, Janata Dal, Nationalist Congress Party and the Indian Union Muslim League.

'I came here in 2005, and understood the great responsibility that comes by being the main imam at such a masjid. Realizing that mischief mongers could spoil a perfectly peaceful atmosphere, we introduced electronic surveillance with CCTVs. As a precaution, we do not allow parking inside the premises at night. We have a zero tolerance policy with respect to terrorism. At the same time, we want the common man to understand what the Quran preaches. So we have a small lecture on the Quran on all working days after Zuhr prayers in the afternoon.'

Muhibullah Nadwi today talks as a seasoned scholar of Islam. This knowledge and expression owes as much to Nadwa and other madrasas he has studied in as the mosques where he has led the prayer in the past.

'Upon passing out of Nadwa, I joined a mosque in Sangam Vihar in Lucknow. I was there for a few months. Then I came to Delhi where I was an imam at Masjid Chand in Abul Fazal Enclave, then another small mosque before coming here. With all the challenges of helming the prayers in a masjid or studying in a madrasa, I would like my daughter who studies in Convent of Jesus and Mary in New Delhi to go to a madrasa, even if for a short time. She should understand the reality of life.'

. . .

Madrasas encourage students to join terrorist ranks: Shia body
—*Deccan Herald*, 9 January 2019

Madrasas give 'education of terrorism': BJP MP Sakshi Maharaj
—*The Economic Times*, 14 September 2014

Ban madrasas to save India from terror: Togadia
—Hindu Jan Jagruti Samiti, 27 February 2009

Darul Uloom Deoband invites Togadia, Katiyar for a visit
—TwoCircles.Net, 14 February 2009

VHP flaps Vajpayee on support to Urdu, madrasas
—*The Times of India*, 23 April 2004

Muslim madrasa students assaulted for not chanting 'Jai Mata Ki'
—India.com, 30 March 2016

8-year-old Madrasa student lynched in South Delhi
—*The Citizen*, 26 October 2018

Madrasas not breeding grounds for terrorism
—*The Hindu*, 30 November 2014

Madrasa children are the most vulnerable
—*The Milli Gazette*, 6 November 2018

Madrasas don't breed people like Godse, Pragya Thakur: Azam Khan
—NDTV, 12 June 2019

A little under two years after Ajay Singh Bisht, popularly known as Yogi Adityanath, took over as the Chief Minister of Uttar Pradesh in March 2017, the chairman of the Shia Central Waqf Board Waseem Rizvi hit the headlines with his claims of madrasas being nurseries of terrorism. In a letter to the Prime Minister Narendra Modi, Rizvi alleged that the madrasas encouraged their students to join the ranks of terrorists, and urged him to close them down. He claimed too that the funds for the madrasas were coming from Pakistan and Bangladesh and 'even some terror outfits were assisting them'. 'If the madrasas are not shut down, half of the Muslims in India will be supporters of IS ideology in next 15 years,' he claimed. With his bagful of wild allegations, Rizvi joined the ranks of Sakshi Maharaj, Member of Parliament, on a Bharatiya Janata Party ticket from Unnao, and Hindutva hotheads like Praveen Togadia and Vinay Katiyar who all have cast aspersions on the integrity of madrasas of India without backing up their allegations with a shred of evidence.

Indeed, what Rizvi said in January 2019, Maharaj had said in 2014 soon after the BJP-led government assumed power. The freshly minted MP alleged,

Education of terrorism is being given in madrasas. It is making them terrorists and jihadis. Muslim youth in madrasas are being motivated for 'love jihad' with offers of cash rewards—₹11 lakh for an affair with a Sikh girl, ₹10 lakh for a Hindu girl and ₹7 lakh for a Jain girl. It is not in national interest. Tell me about one madrasa where tricolour is hoisted even on August 15 and January 26.

Maharaj did not substantiate his allegations with evidence. Nor was he asked by the media to share the source of the remunerative figures he had arrived. While the media somewhat conveniently dismissed his words as the ranting of a fringe element, he was taken seriously in the ruling party circles.

Almost on cue, among the first things that Adityanath did after becoming the Chief Minister was to ask the madrasas to hoist the Tricolour on 15 August and record the proceedings of Independence Day functions. The recording, in turn, was to be submitted to the government. This seemingly innocuous order actually stemmed from an underlying suspicion that the madrasas are not quite nationalist as also the desire to project them as dens of anti-nationals. After all, similar orders were not passed by the administration for the Rashtriya Swayamsevak Sangh (RSS)-run schools in the state. It may be recalled, the RSS did not hoist the Tricolour for more than 50 years after Independence, preferring its own *bhagwa* dhwaj. And immediately after Independence, it was not some madrasa students but the activists of the RSS who trampled over the Tricolour. Pertinently, while the first President of India, Dr Rajendra Prasad, had studied in a madrasa, the terrorist responsible for taking the life of Mahatma Gandhi, Nathuram Godse had joined the RSS in 1932.

While it is highly unlikely that any of the politicians would have spent time studying about the madrasas, the media too has been both irresponsible and indifferent, casting insidious aspersions on the entire community. Journalists who would not have set foot in a madrasa once in their lifetime have taken to filing reams and reams on the functioning of madrasas. In a classic case of motivated journalism, they set out with preconceived notions and age-old prejudice to show madrasas as the den of terror. About such venom, Yoginder Sikand wrote in *Bastions of the Believers*,

> In the absence of any comprehensive knowledge of madrasas, and goaded by prejudice and preconceived notions, journalists and writers with their own agenda to pursue have been quick to link the madrasas with radical Islamist movements and to brand them indiscriminately as 'dens of terror' allegedly churning out legions of fanatic 'warriors of Islam'.

However, it will be both unfair and inaccurate to claim that such allegations on the madrasas have been levelled only after 'Hindu Hriday Samrat' Narendra Modi became the Prime Minister. The fact is this insidious campaign has been on for almost two decades.

All that has changed are the names and parties of those levelling allegations. The substance of their claims remains the same: Madrasas are dens of terrorism! If after 2014, we have had a Rizvi or a Maharaj saying it, earlier the likes of Vinay Katiyar and Praveen Togadia mouthed predictable insinuations. Back in February 2009, Togadia had said in a public address in Kerala, 'Madrasas should be banned to save India from terror'. In much the same way, Katiyar said, 'The madrasas should be investigated, the source of their funds should be investigated.'

Interestingly, while the allegations, all unsubstantiated, remain the same, but are hurled repeatedly, the defence too is almost a carbon copy. If in 2009, in response to Togadia's claims, the Darul Uloom, Deoband authorities invited him to spend some time in the seminary to understand its philosophy of peace and patriotism, in 2019, in response to Rizvi's claims, the All India Muslim Personal Law Board spokesman Khalilur Rehman talked of the key role played in the freedom movement by madrasas. 'By raising questions on madrasas, Rizvi was insulting them,' he said.

Indeed, even Sachar Committee Report alluded to such misgivings. Rubbishing the contention, the report said,

> It is often believed that a large proportion of Muslim children study in Madarsas, mostly to get acquainted with the religious discourse and ensure the continuation of Islamic culture and social life. A persistent belief nurtured…. It is also argued that education in Madarsas often encourages religious fundamentalism and creates a sense of alienation from the mainstream. In actuality the number of Madarsa attending students is much less than commonly believed. For example, in West Bengal, where Muslims form 25% of the population, the number of Madarsa students at 3.41 lakhs is only about 4% of the 7–19 age group. NCAER figures indicate that only about 4% of all Muslim students of the school going age group are enrolled in Madarsas. At the all-India level this works out to be about 3% of all Muslim children of school going age…. One reason for the misconception that

the majority of Muslim children are enrolled in Madarsas is that people do not distinguish between Madarsas and Maktabs. While Madarsas provide education (religious and/ or regular), the Maktabs are neighbourhood schools, often attached to mosques, that provide religious education to children who attend other schools to get 'mainstream' education. Thus Maktabs provide part-time religious education and are complementary to the formal educational institutions. The common belief that a high proportion of Muslim children study in Madarsas stems from the fact that they are actually enrolled in the local Maktabs. As emphasized, such local Maktabs provide not a substitute, but a supplementary educational service. In Kerala, for instance, more than 60,000 Muslim students study in both 'mainstream' institutions and Maktabs at the same time. Since private and Government-aided schools do not teach Urdu adequately, children have to be taught to read the scriptures at home. Some children are taught to read the Holy Quran by their parents, relatives or by private tutors. In many cases, especially in low and medium income families, parents do not have the time or ability to teach their children themselves. Micro-level studies show that such parents admit their children to maktabs, in addition to secular schools. In such cases, the children study in two schools. Based on the NCERT (provisional) data the percentage of Muslim children aged 7–19 years going to the first type of maktabs has been estimated. Even these figures are not very high—only 4% of Muslim children study in them. While this percentage is lower in urban areas, interestingly it is almost the same between boys and girls.

With a vast majority of Muslims preferring government or public schools, madrasas cater largely to first-generation learners. It is this segment that needs the most encouragement to pursue education. Yet, the madrasas, which are a convenient and cost-effective first school for children from such families, face the ire of the larger Indian society. Politicians of many hues, and even political commentators spread the notion that the madrasas somehow are opposed to nationalism, and are veritable dens of terror. It is this preconceived notion that has resulted in ruining the life of many a madrasa student or teacher. This is not to say no madrasa student/teacher has ever been guilty of wrongdoing— just in May 2019, a madrasa teacher was nabbed for criminal assault on a 12-year-old girl. In another instance, a cleric in a madrasa beat a six-year-old girl with a leather belt for failing to pronounce a word correctly. After a non-cognizable report was registered in Noida, the cleric disappeared. Fortunately, such incidents are few, and usually immediately dealt with by the law enforcing agencies. The madrasas strike public conscience whenever there is a terrorist attack, or even something which appears to be a terrorist attack. Then the needle of suspicion is pointed towards madrasas. It matters not a bit to the media that the madrasas do not talk in terms of changing the political system nor do they teach about jihad. If at all any mention is made of jihad, it is of the pacific kind, the one that involves control over one's passion and desire rather than hatred towards non-Muslims. But the media and the politicians seldom bother to find out the truth. A university student nabbed for a public attack never has his college's name attached to his name in headlines. A madrasa student merely accused of terrorism is always identified as a product of the madrasa system of education. Different folks, different strokes. At the end of it all, it is the innocent who suffer.

Take for instance the sorry case of Mujibur Rahman who studied at a madrasa in Yavatmal in Maharashtra and later rose to be an imam at the local Jama Masjid. Mujibur Rahman, then aged 23, got married in 2013. A product of Madrasa Jamia Ishaatul Quran in Pusad, Yavatmal district, he looked forward to a life of dignity and progress. Soon he was blessed with a son too. As he became an imam at the local Jama Masjid, Mujibur Rahman in his own limited way felt a sense of contentment.

Then came Eid ul Azha or Bakra Eid on 25 September 2015, and his life came apart. On the fateful day, a young man Abdul Malik Abdul Razzaq attacked the police just outside the Eidgah for alleg-edly enforcing beef ban. A scuffle ensued. The man was arrested.

The police contended that the man attacked them with a knife, and also two others who tried to prevent him from assaulting the policemen. During interrogation, the police claimed to have found that he was influenced by some jihadis. So the case was transferred to the Anti-Terrorism Squad (ATS). During probe, police arrested Mujib and another man Shoeb for influencing Abdul Malik to carry out unlawful activities. Mujib was alleged to have made hate speeches. The police arrested both Mujib and Shoeb and slapped Unlawful Activities Prevention Act (UAPA) on them. They were acquitted only in May 2019 by the sessions court in Akola, Maharashtra.

Mujib says,

> Though I got bail, I spent 18 days in police and judicial custody. The police inflicted torture during the custody. They abused me, spoke lies about my family to mentally torture me. I am a patient so they did not carry out as much torture as they are known to do. But even then I was not given the medical care that my condition warranted. I passed out of Madrasa Jamia Ishaatul Quran which is run by Jamaat-e-Islami Hind, and later did my BA from Maulana Azad National Urdu University in Hyderabad. I am an imam at the Jama Masjid, but I was put to such indignity for no fault of mine.

Adding to this, during the time he was away, his wife was dependent on financial aid from the Jamaat and other well-wishers. 'It was nice of the Jamaat and others, but nobody likes to live on charity. What was my fault that I was arrested? They probably wanted somebody who looked like a Muslim. Anyway, I am grateful that my honour has been restored now.'

Mujib is the not the only one. Shoeb who was arrested alongside Mujib had a similarly harrowing tale to relate. He too alleged he was tortured in custody by the ATS and pressured to make false statements. Well-respected site scroll.in exposed the media's coverage of the arrest of Mujib and Shoeb. It said,

Pusad town in eastern Maharashtra made headlines in September 2015 when news emerged that a young Muslim man had stabbed three policemen with a kitchen knife, allegedly in rage over the beef ban introduced that year. Twenty-year-old Abdul Malik's arrest was followed a month later by two other men in the region being arrested: Shoeb Khan, 28, from Hingoli and Maulana Mujeebur Rahman from Yavatmal.... Soon, reports appeared in newspapers describing Khan, Malik and Mujeebur Rahman as radicalised youth involved with the Islamic State or ISIS. The Times of India described their arrest as the 'crippling' of a 'terror module in the making'. Nearly four years later, the three men have been cleared of all terror-related charges.[1]

There have been others like Salman Farsi who too was falsely implicated in the Malegaon blast case. Also there is Mufti Abdul Qayyum who was accused of being behind the Akshardham attack.

Soon after the attack on the Indian Parliament, the Akshardham attack in Gujarat on 24 September 2002, in which 32 people died, grabbed national and international headlines. For a layman, it seemed terrorists had laid siege to the country, every institution was at risk. As our electronic media flashed the photographs of men with skullcaps and long, flowing beards as the men behind the attack, the image made an instant impact on the minds of the viewers. 'That is what a terrorist looks like', was the unsaid but not unexpressed sentiment. Among those whose photograph was widely circulated on our television screens without any qualification of 'an alleged terrorist', or 'claimed to be a terrorist by the police' was Mufti Abdul Qayyum Mansuri.

Following the Akshardham attack in which he falsely implicated, he spent more than a decade in the jail before he was

---

[1] https://scroll.in/article/925362/special-report-my-life-is-ruined-says-muslim-man-acquitted-of-terror-charges-after-4-years-in-ja

acquitted by the honourable Supreme Court in May 2014. The three-judge Bench of the apex court stated that 'Fiction must make sense'. It was an open indictment of the malicious motives and the final work of the investigators. The court observed,

> One needs to express anguish at the incompetence with which the investigating agencies conducted the investigation of the case of such a grievous nature, involving the integrity and security of the nation. Instead of booking the real culprits responsible for taking so many previous lives, the police caught innocent people, and framed grievous charges against them which resulted in their convictions and subsequent sentencing. We intend to take note of the perversity in conducting this case at various stages, right from the investigation level to the granting of sanction by the state government to prosecute the accused persons under POTA, the conviction and awarding the sentence. We, being the apex court, cannot afford to sit with folded hands when such gross violation of fundament rights and basic human rights of the citizens of this country is presented before us. There is a need to reinvestigate the dreaded terror attack and unveil real culprits.

Mansuri though penned his ordeal in an Urdu and Gujarati book about a year after he was acquitted. Titled *Eleven Years behind the Bars*, he wrote about how the security agencies manipulated the law, and framed the innocent. In his book, he claimed, he was given the 'choice' of being implicated in any of the three cases related to the burning of the train in Godhra, Haren Pandya's murder in Gujarat or the attack on Akshardham.

He wrote in his book,

> For three days and nights, they made me copy a letter that they had given me. They (the police) would bring an expert each day to check whether I had copied it well. They would ask me to copy the twists and turns of the Urdu letters so that they looked exactly the same, as in the letter. They had beaten me

to pulp. Even took me out to stage an encounter. I was very afraid, and did what they told me to do.

Adding further, 'Then they claimed in court that I had written the letters.' Incidentally, the main charge against him was that the two letters, recovered from the two suicide attackers, were written by him. Fortunately, for Mansuri, the prosecution failed to substantiate how the letters remained unsoiled and unstained when the bodies of the fidayeen—ripped with bullets—were soiled in mud and blood.

That was like divine help. Otherwise, the time he was in jail, his life changed forever. His father passed away, his family had to move to another house.

His story runs parallel to that of Dr Salman Farsi, an imam and a hafiz who spent seven years in a madrasa before becoming a Unani doctor. He was accused of abetting in the crime and conspiracy of Malegaon serial blasts. The blasts that occurred soon after the Friday prayers near the Hamidiya Masjid on 8 September 2006, killed more than 30 and left more than 125 injured. The ATS arrested nine Muslim men, including Dr Farsi. After being picked up on 5 November 2006, he was to spend the next five years in Maharashtra jails before being granted bail in 2011. And then he had to wait for another five years before being absolved. In April 2016, a sessions court discharged Dr Farsi and all other accused Muslim men of all terror charges in the case. Sessions Judge V. V. Patil declared that the eight men be 'set at liberty'—the ninth accused, Shabbir Ahmed, had passed away. Criticizing the ATS for the arrests, Patil said,

In my view, the basic foundation or the objective shown by ATS behind the blast is not acceptable to a man of ordinary prudence. I say so because there was 'Ganesh immersion' just prior to September 8, 2006.... Had accused no. 1 to 9 any objective that there should be riots at Malegaon, then they ought to have planted bombs at the time of Ganesh immersion which would have caused death of most Hindu people. It seems to me highly impossible that accused no. 1 to 9 who are from Muslim communities, that too on a holy day, i.e., Shab-e Barat. (Sessions Judge V. V. Patil's judgement, April 2016)

It is pertinent to remember Dr Farsi is a hafiz and has been an imam as well. Inside the jail, he used to lead the Friday prayers and also the special prayers on Eid. When he was released, his life had changed beyond belief. He could no longer carry on with his medical practice as he had the stigma of a terrorist attached to his name.

Now think about the allegations of the media, and the irresponsible statements of the politicians. The media, after every unfortunate attack, rather than questioning the investigating agencies about their lapses, goes to town with photographs of the innocent as the terrorists. In the mind of the common man it reinforces the stereotypes of the madrasas being the breeding grounds of terrorism, as happened in the case of Dr Farsi and Mufti Mansuri. The truth could not be farther from the allegation as all the subsequent acquittals have proved.

It, however, is not a recent occurrence. Many years ago when the UPA was in power (2004–2014) innocent men were routinely rounded up, arrested, tortured in custody before being found innocent by the court. S. M. Mushrif, former Inspector General of Police, Maharashtra, talked of a number of such cases, ranging from Ajmer Sharif (2007) blast, Mecca Masjid blasts (2007) and Samjhauta Express blasts (2007) to German bakery (2010) and Dulsukhnagar bomb blasts (2013) in his painstakingly researched book *Brahminists Bombed, Muslims Hanged*. Though Mushrif cast his net beyond the madrasas to the community in general, this blame game of the innocent has been carrying on longer still. It has its roots in the 9/11 attack on the Twin Towers in 2001, and the alleged role of al-Qaeda behind it. Following the deadly blasts, it was widely believed that madrasas had at least some role, even if not pivotal, in the tragedy. Writes Muhammadullah Khalili Qasmi in *Madrasa Education,*

Since Al-Qaeda was believed to be based in Afghanistan where, at that time, the Taliban were in power who attributed themselves to madrasas of Deobandi school of thought in Pakistan, So with Taliban every madrasa, especially in South Asia, came under the shadow of doubt and from where the madrasas were branded as centres of fundamentalism and terrorism.

Though none of the 18 hijackers were a madrasa product—all had studied in the West, some even in the USA—the impression lingered. This is despite the fact that the former President of Afghanistan Burhanuddin Rabbani, scoffing at such allegations, saying, 'It is a propaganda. None of those who are labelled as terrorists is a product of a madrasa. Osama bin Laden himself is an engineer and his deputy a doctor.' Well-known Islamic scholar saw in the constant running down of the madrasas a larger design, a 'long-hatched conspiracy'. He wrote,

Every just man who will realize the new campaign against madrasas in the global perspective he will come to a conclusion that it is a weapon that the West has adopted to curb them and lessen the growing trends to Islamic education. After the defeat of Communism, the West is readying to fight the Islamic world. The policy-makers of the West have dug the reason that madrasas are the fountainheads from where Islamic society gets life and energy.

Incidentally, around the time of 9/11, India was being governed by the Bharatiya Janata Party-led National Democratic Alliance. Never known for nursing a positive attitude towards the madrasas, the opportunity came as a blessing for the more radical elements within the ruling dispensation. The then Minister of State for Home Vidyasagar Rao came up with his own theory of suspicion and panic, stating there were 31,850 madrasas in the country. Of these, 11,453 were in the border areas, and hence susceptible to the influence of Pakistan's ISI. On 10 April 2002, he contended that 'terrorist activities' were taking place in 'some madrasas' in Kerala. Two weeks later, a Parliamentary Standing

Committee on Home Affairs sought 'strict action against religious fundamentalist institutions which have come up in the country, particularly along India–Nepal border, with the help of Pakistan ISI for indoctrinating young minds to wage holy war against India.' About a year before the committee's report, a Group of Ministers of the Government of India had released a report on national security. Titled 'Reforming the National Security System', it was prepared by a four-member team, led by L. K. Advani. It identified madrasas as a source of threat to national security. The report sought to link the rise of Taliban to the possibility of its growth in India:

> The Taliban success in Afghanistan brought about a qualitative change in the security environment of the region. It also gave rise to groups of Jihadi forces. These forces were unlikely to stop in Afghanistan and Pakistan. These bands of religious fanatics are indulging in subversive activities and have expansionist designs. They will work relentlessly for the break up of the Indian Union.

This was the first time that irregular madrasas were dubbed as illegal madrasas, quietly erasing the rights of the minorities to run educational institutions of their choice. Noted author Yoginder SIkand noted in *The Indian State and the Madrasa*,

> Ever since the Bharatiya Janata party-led coalition assumed office at the Centre in India, there has been a spate of attacks on Muslim madrasas, mosques and dargahs, in various parts of the country. Senior Hindutva leaders, within and outside the government, have issued statements alleging that the Pakistan secret service agency, the Inter-Services Intelligence has infiltrated numerous madrasas all over the country, particularly in districts along the country's borders with Pakistan, Nepal and Bangladesh. A detailed report of the Indian intelligence agencies claims that some of these madrasas are training grounds for ISI spies and anti-Indian 'terrorists'. The report goes on to suggest that the muftis, maulvis and imams in these

religious schools may have been replaced by what it calls 'highly fanatic agents of ISI'.

This trait of looking at madrasas, particularly those in the border areas, itself drew fuel from the teachings of the Hindutva ideologue Deen Dayal Upadhyay who wanted a 10-mile corridor along the border with Pakistan from where the Muslims would be expelled.

From 2001 to present, the needle of suspicion is pointed at madrasas as the dens of terror. No evidence is ever provided. While the madrasas continue to teach their pupils under the shadow of fear, it has made life that bit more difficult for the innocent students. As Mohammed Ali (see biosketches) discovered to his dismay on his way to his madrasa in Pilibhit in Uttar Pradesh.

Salman Farsi, a Quran Hafiz, was falsely implicated in the Malegaon blast case

What needs to be done is to tell the common man about the role of the madrasas in the spread of elementary education in the country where one-third of the population still cannot read or write. It is critical to bring out the reality of the madrasas in India. While some like Darul Uloom, Deoband, have played a critical role in the freedom struggle of India—the Deoband school acted as an effective counter to the divisive ways of the Muslim League—others, including thousands of nondescript madrasas with all their obvious limitations, have imparted at least elementary knowledge to that segment of the population which not only cannot afford to give education to its children, but is also unable to give two square meals. Much before the Government of India came up with the Midday Meal Scheme to encourage more children to come to school, madrasas had been offering three meals a day to its residential students.

As for Rizvi, Togadia and their ilk, a quick trip to any madrasa will cure them of prejudice and ignorance. Far from being the breeding ground of terrorism or places where separatist tendencies are nurtured, madrasas suffer from acute shortage of resources, infrastructure, manpower and so on. Unsung heroes for some, untamed villains for others, the role of the madrasas has not been understood by most.

Our Lord, give us in this world that which is good,
and in the Hereafter that which is good,
and save us from the torment of the Fire.

**—VERSE 201, SURAH BAQARAH,
THE QURAN**

Chapter 2

REMINISCENCES OF A UTOPIAN PAST

First Madrasas during the Time of the Prophet

Madrasa is an Arabic word (the plural being Madaris, similar to masajid for a masjid or mosque), which literally, as per the roots, means school; a place where people get *dars* (lesson). In secondary meaning, which is in vogue, it is a place where Islamic religious education is imparted. The transformation of Madrasa from its literal meaning to its current avatar is the history of Muslim's education system in a nutshell. That history of Muslim education is still one of the comparatively dark areas is something on which most historians agree. This is partly due to lack of sufficient original sources and partly due to the less than desired attention of native and foreign historians.

The coming into being of a madrasa is a protracted phase of an evolution rather than creation. Left to its own, every child learns a lot from his or her surroundings. As per their potential, parents impart some knowledge and hence become first tutors. The well-off parents engage tutor (mu'addib) for their children who would provide tarbiya (training) and make them learn languages, particularly Arabic and Persian and teach reading of Quran. Those people who did travelling (rihlah) to acquire knowledge were always the sought-after lot by rulers and wealthy families. More often than not, these people would do group teachings called majlis or halqa in mosques. If in a locality there were more of such people, each would hold separate majalis or halqa in the same mosques at different timings and as per their specialization. Hence, we had Tafseer halqa, Hadees halqa or Fiqh halqa. This was the first semi-organized teaching or learning institution which emerged during the period of Prophet Mohammad. The Prophet himself used the house of Zaid bin Arqam, called 'Dar-ul-Arqam' in Makkah, near the famous hillock of Safa, to teach those who had accepted Islam. Later on when the Prophet migrated to Madina and when the now famous mosque Al-Masjid Al-Nabavi was built, at its eastern side a platform named Suffa was built for education and training purpose. It was probably the first instance of a madrasa operating out of a masjid.

'Islamic' education which was imparted to those who had accepted Islam was different from the type of education or rather literacy prevalent in pre-Prophet Arabia. Poetry, which was composed to praise their family, tribe and gods, was the main literary form, they loved to excel at. For them it was the record of knowledge 'Diwan ul-Ilm' and the highest expression of wisdom 'Muntaha ul-Hikma'. Despite the high esteem in which ancient Arab poetry was held even after the revival of Islam by its last prophet, Prophet Muhammad, the Quran refers to this era as the age of Jahiliyya, of stubbornness, of refusal to reason, logic or new ideas, hence ignorance. This period was marked by polytheism, individual fulfilment, tribal biases, anarchy, crudeness, barbarism, particularly towards women. Islam brought the message of sharing and caring, respect and love for all, equal status for women, no exploitation of poor, weak and needy. Its first divine decree, the first revealed verse asks followers to 'Read with the name (and attributes) of the sustainer who created'. Thus, acquisition of knowledge is linked with the attributes of the Creator, which are nothing but all niceties.

From the semi-organized structures of Majlis and Halqa, emerged Maktab and Madrasa. The former, also called 'Kuttab', was meant to remove illiteracy and provide teachings of the Quran along with grammar, prose, poetry, history, etc. These were held in houses, shops or any other place, including a mosque and were headed by a mu'allim. Madrasas were institutions of secondary and higher learning. Their main features varied from region to region or community but all were residential with Arabic as the medium of instruction. They relied on oral and aural communication between teacher and taught. The main components of their curricula were Arabic grammar, Tafsir (exegesis), Fiqh (jurisprudence), Hadith (Prophet's sayings), Usul-ul-Fiqh (principles of jurisprudence), Usu-ul-Hadith (principles of narration) and life sketch of the Prophet and Sahaba (the companions). Besides, classical sciences like astronomy, mathematics, geography and medicine and Arabic literature were also taught in most of the madrasas.

It is understandable that with a wide variety of subjects to teach and to specialize in, different scholars and their groups chose different areas. Fiqh or jurisprudence was an emerging choice as it connected scholars directly with people as they were approached for solutions of problems related to day-to-day work, business and relationships. It was a source of better income. This 'orthodox' group gradually excluded philosophy and sciences from curricula of their madrasas and thus was the beginning of bifurcation of knowledge in madrasas. By 12th century, a rigid system of Muslims higher education had emerged: (a) 'unrestricted institutions' such as the Jamia (Jami) and certain other centres of study and open discussion; (b) 'exclusive institutions' represented by Madrasas. Both had their own patrons who supported them.

A welcome exception to this trend was the establishment of an unrestricted Madrasa in 631 AH by Al- Mustansir, the last but one of the Abbasid Caliphs, which was open to students of all major orthodox schools. However, it remained a one of a kind of exception and never became a trend setter that could reverse the increasing exclusionist approach of madrasas. A historic example of this exclusionism and its reaction is the group of madrasas established by Saljuq Vazir Nizam ul mulk all over the Saljuq empire. The main purpose of these 'Nizamiya' Madrasas was to spread Sunni ideology and to counter and restrict Shia (Shi'ite) Madrasas. They were established in Basra, Baghdad, Mosul, Mesopotamia, Marv, Herat and Balkh. Most prominent among these was the one built in Baghdad in 1065 AD. It attracted best of the brains of that time and had a large collection of books.

In University of Al-Qarawiyyin we see an example of a Jamia along with a madrasa, established in 859 AD. This university situated in Fez, Morocco was unique in more than one way. It was the first Islamic educational institution established by a lady, Fatima al-Fihri with an associated madrasa. She was the daughter of a wealthy merchant Mohammed Al-Fihri. The family migrated from Kairouan in Tunisia to Fez in early 9th century. Fatima and her sister Mariam, both of whom were well educated, inherited a fortune from their father and decided to put it to some good use. Mariam used most of her share to build the central mosque that can house about 22,000 people for praying. Fatima spent all of her money, time and energy to construct the university and madrasa. It is the oldest existing university in the world, according to UNESCO and Guinness Book of World Records, functioning since more than 1,000 years. In 1963, it was incorporated into Morocco's State University system. Famous alumni who have studied here include renowned Muslim philosopher Ibn-e-Rushd, Latinized as Averroes and Pope Sylvester II who is said to have introduced Arabic numerals to Europe after studying here in 10th century.

Al-Qarawiyyin Library which contains some of the oldest pre-served manuscripts is now one of the most important resource centres for researchers, particularly after destruction of libraries in other Arab nations, like Iraq's Mosul university library, during recent decades.

From the University of Al-Qarawiyyin to Darul Uloom, the faithful have come a long way. It, however, begs a question: why could not all subsequent madrasas be more like Al-Qarawiyyin?

The Concept of *Ilm* in Islam

We all know madrasas, whatever their orientation, are supposed to spread knowledge, or 'ilm'. The Quran asks us to pursue knowledge. We pray to almighty to increase our knowledge, as a verse of the Quran says. But what is 'ilm'? Is it limited to mere reading or memorization of the Quran, as many of our madrasas tend to believe and preach? Or does it have wider ramifications? According to the dictionaries, the meaning of science or 'ilm' is to know something deservedly, to recognize, to perceive reality, to acquire belief, to feel and to learn firmly (*taaj-ul-uroos wa muheet-ul-muheet*). Likewise, the one who perceives reality is called 'aalim' whose plural comes to be 'aalimoon'. And the plural of 'aleem' is 'ulamaa', that is, those having deep and firm knowledge. The term ulamma is what we tend to use for scholars of Islam. A basic meaning of this is like a unique mark on something which distinguishes itself from the others (*maqaayees al-lughah. Ibn e faris*).

The Quran has declared 'hearing', 'sight' and 'heart' as the means of acquiring knowledge (that is the essential medium for attaining faith). At another place 'fuad' is also termed in place of 'qalb' (Surah Bani-Israel, verse 36). This includes both, knowledge by perceptual and conceptual means. And with respect to 'fuad', it also includes senses. But because knowledge can be called as knowledge only when it reaches up to the level of belief, the Quran has termed revelation as knowledge and its antonym as heretics (Surah Al-Baqarah, verse 120), that is, human self-made imaginations and emotional devotions for which he does not have any justification or evidence. This is the reason the Quran emphasizes very much on acquiring knowledge about external universe. Because the basis of this type of knowledge is upon justifications and evidence, and upon realities and proofs. Emotional devotion is not involved in this at all. It presents every claim of it, with the strength of justification and evidence, and also asks for justifications and evidence from those who deny these claims. It has so much belief in the firmness of its claims (and belief comes into being by knowledge) that it proclaims about those who deny these claims, that they cannot present any evidence in denial (Surah Al-Mominoon, verse 117). This is why the invitation of Quran is 'upon-visuality-reason' invitation (Surah Yusuf, verse 108), namely it is rational.

'Aalam' has been derived from this matter (plural of which is 'aalameen'). The noun specifically used for tools 'ism-e-aalah' has also got a derivative 'subject' like 'khaatam ma yukhtamu bihi. qaalab. ma yuqlabu bihi', etc., 'Aalam' is also like this which means 'ma yu'lamu bihi', that is, a substance by means of which knowledge of something is acquired. Because the knowledge of God is acquired by means of universe, the whole universe is called 'aalam'. Furthermore, all among different sides and corners of the universe will be called as 'aalam'; for example, the 'human world', 'water world', 'fire world', etc. The reason for making its 'masculine unchanged plural' (the plural made by addition of letters at the end of its singular where the original singular word remains unchanged) is that human is also included in it. And when in a word some other creature is also included with humans, then human is kept dominant. That is why a generation or nation is also called 'aalam' (and also decade and century). The Quran has often used 'aalameen' in the meaning of nations, or coexistent humans of some age. From this direction 'rabb ul aalameen' means sustainer of the whole universe, in which humans will also be included.

God's attribute of being the Lord of the worlds (*rabb ul aalameen*) should appear in perceivable and apparent form. It should not remain merely as a visual image or belief. This can develop the state of praise 'hamd'.

Now let us examine the Quran's way of describing 'ilm':

The Quran states, 'allama aadam alasmaau kullaha' (Surah Al-Baqarah, verse 31) meaning Allah granted man the knowledge of everything in the universe. Or 'allam al insaana ma lam yaalam' (Surah Al-Alaq, verse 5) meaning He taught human what he did not know. And He taught him (writing) through the pen—'allama bil qalam' (Surah Al-Alaq, verse 4). These verses do not mean that God has taught every human exactly the way a teacher teaches a child. Its meaning is that Allah has put capability of these things in human beings. Granted them their capacity. Its clear example is found in Surah Maidah where it is stated that you teach (to catch prey) your hunting dogs 'mimma allamakum Allah' (Surah Al-Maidah, verse 4) by virtue of the knowledge that Allah has bestowed upon you. It is clear that Allah does not teach the way of training a hunting animal to a human. He has put its capacity in a human by which he himself acquires this knowledge.

Thus one type of knowledge is what prophet gets directly from God. That is called revelation or 'vahi'. And the second type of knowledge's capacity has been put in all the humans, and whoever wishes can acquire it. This difference is necessary to be regarded—that is, the difference of level of knowledge acquired through revelation and through human capacity. The same difference exists in prophet's knowledge. One knowledge that he gets by means of revelation in which no one other than the prophet is associated. And his other knowledge is human capacity in which his status is not of a prophet, (but) of a (common) mortal. This is the status in which he has been ordered to consult others (Surah Aale-Imran, verse 159).

Now let us examine the verse of Surah Al-Baqarah in which grant of the knowledge 'al-Asmaa kullaha' (all the names) to Adam, that is human being, is mentioned. The expression 'asmaa' is plural of 'ism' whose matter (root) is 'seen-meem-waao'. The meaning of 'ism' is a symbol of something by which it can be recognized. Here the Surah Al Baqarah verse means that 'Adam' (man) has been given such ability about knowledge of things that he gives name to everything for recognizing it by knowing its appearance and characteristics. Analyse that human brain works in a similar way, that it understands everything by its characteristics and recognizes it through its name. When a child starts the process of getting acquainted with the environment around him, he recognizes things around him by their appearance, by their odour and taste, or by their sounds. He smiles and gets attentive on familiar sounds, recognizes odour of his mother. Later he learns the names of them and puts labels such as this is 'mother', and this is 'father' or 'dad'. As he grows, he understands, this globe of glass on the ceiling, which gives light in the evening is called 'bulb'. Though if you tell the name of a thing even to an adult and intelligent man, with which he is not 'acquainted', neither will he be able to understand it, nor will he be able to make an image of it in his mind. However, when he will get 'acquaintance' of that thing, that is, he will get knowledge of that, it will be added to his mind. The same is the matter with 'asmaa' of 'Rabb' (names of God). If we are just acquainted with the names of Allah but are unaware of His nature's charisma, and the scenes and mementos spread over the universe, then obligation of acquaintance is not discharged. 'Bismillah' (with the name of Allah) remains just verbal. Starting a task with the name of Allah has the peculiarity that, at that moment you also remember Allah's attributes along with His name. The glimpse of Allah's attributes is sighted in His universe, seen in His signs. For understanding which, getting acquaintance with them is essential and the key of acquaintance with them is in 'uloom' (plural of knowledge). It is in 'ilm ul aayat' (knowledge of verses/signs, both in the Quran and in the Universe).

In the mentioned verse, the word 'kullaha' is very important and noteworthy. This one word has given an invitation to humans for becoming familiar with the huge ocean of knowledge. That is, Allah has put capacity in human to acquire knowledge of everything, this is now upon his discretion and ability that how much portion of it can he acquire. How does he pass over these grades of insight. Its extremely notable form appears in the mentioned verse of Surah Al-Baqarah where Allah says that He has granted Adam the knowledge of all things in universe and it is mentioned in Surah Al-Nahl that 'Allah has brought you out of the wombs of your mothers in a condition that you did not know anything'. He gave you ears, eyes and (thinking) hearts so that you become thankful (Surah Al-Nahl, verse78). As though when human being came into the world, he did not have knowledge of anything. However, Allah had granted him ear, eye and ability to think so that with the help of these tools he could acquire knowledge of Allah's universe. If he, in this way, acquires knowledge of Allah's universe, then it will be a practical acknowledgement for the blessings, which have been granted to him because their use will then exactly be according to Allah's will.

Notable thing is that when knowledge and acquiring knowledge is discussed, majority of us term it as 'religious studies'. Worldly studies are left out of religion and just for 'worldly gains', whereas the truth is that 'ilm' is a word of Arabic language. 'Almaurid' which in English–Arabic as well as Arabic–English authentic dictionary translates 'ilm' (علم) as 'science'.

Here it is also necessary to understand that science is not the name of a subject as usually understood, like physics, chemistry. Science is actually the name of a progression or methodology, 'tareeqat'. What method do we use for becoming aware from unaware. If we try to understand the truth by observation, by thinking on overview results, by research on that, and wherever possible by experiments, then this is the scientific method, and this is what is called science and this is the method of acquiring knowledge according to the Quran, becoming aware from un-aware. The Quran emphasizes observation, hearing, thinking (hearing, vision, heart) and also talks about accountability on the Day of Judgment upon the use of these blessings. Further clarity about the same meaning of knowledge and science can be acquired by seeing the display board at any Arabic university's faculty of science where 'kulliyat ul uloom' would be found written. Mentioned in Surah Al-Fatir, verses 27–28,

> Haven't you thought over the truth that Allah makes the rain from clouds and from that grows different types of fruits and (see that how) in mountains white and red terrains (or classes) exist which have different types and a few among them are very black. And similarly there are also different types in humans, in other living things, and in cattle.

Here with much clarity the Quran has mentioned those studies which in modern terminology are called pure science studies. After that 'innama yakhshallaha min ibaadihil ulamaa...'it is the truth that among His mortals only those remain anxious in front (of mastery and greatness) of Him, who are 'Ulamaa'— Knowledgeable among his mortals. Due to this knowledge and recognition they are well aware of Allah's greatness and therefore are anxious of Him. This is the truth and definition of 'ilm', which is proven by dictionaries and the Quran. Under this light, can our madrasas still insist on exclusion of the so-called modern sciences, or even a vertical division of the sacred and the secular ilm? The answer is blowing in the wind.

Madrasas in Medieval India

Alauddin Khilji (1296–1316) was a rare Sultanate ruler, maybe even among the greatest rulers India has had. He united the country from the north to the south. Much before India's Independence in 1947, he united the country. Under him, the first two decades of the 14th century saw a single formidable ruler from Delhi to Madurai. Gujarat and central India were conquered as also a good part of the Deccan and southern India, embracing the kingdoms of the Yadavas of Devagiri, the Kakatiyas of Warangal, the Hoysalas of Dwarsamudra and the Pandyas of Madurai. It was the biggest, in fact, real Indian empire for the first time since the Mauryas. Alauddin, however, was not a practising Muslim. Almost all his decisions were based on his administrative and political acumen, and not guided by the shariah. As noted historian Mohammed Habib wrote in *Studies in Medieval Indian Politics and Culture*,

> The greatest ruler that the Musalmans of India have produced neither fasted nor prayed. He never went to the Friday congregation…. He was hundred per cent Indian; he had never been to foreign lands. He knew nothing about the Shariat, and did not care to go to it for guidance. He was neither afraid of meeting death nor reluctant in inflicting it…the sole object of Alauddin's policy was 'service of the people of God'.

Indeed, Alauddin was a rare Sultanate ruler. Not known for fondness for the written word, some even believed he could not even say Friday prayers. Understandably, he was not indulgent towards ulemma or madrasas. It was in stark contrast to some of the rulers who preceded him, and many who succeeded him. Indeed, the whimsical Tughlaq ruler Mohammed bin Tughlaq (1325–1351) was known for his ability to recite the Quran faultlessly. Firoz Tughlaq (1351–1388) was never lacking in encouragement for men of letters. Even the first Tughlaq, Ghiyasuddin (1320–1325) to whom the widely respected saint Nizamuddin Auliya famously said, 'Hunuz! Dilli door ast' (the Tughlaq ruler who was on his way to Delhi to punish the Sufi perished on the way with the collapse of a bridge) quite liked and respected Amir Khusrau, close confidant and friend of Auliya. Incidentally, Auliya did not exactly have the best of relations with the kings. Yet it never meant pupils could not gather at his hospices, and learn from him. As Raziuddin Aquil writes in *Lovers of God: Sufism and the Politics of Islam in Medieval India*,

> It is said that once Auliya was asked to attend the court of Sultan Qutb-ud-din who, after the death of the Khalji king Alauddin, had killed the heir apparent Khizr Khan, a disciple of Nizamuddin. His refusal to do so enraged the sultan who immediately declared if he did not come to attend the court on the first of the following month, he would have him brought forcibly. When the saint was informed, he went to the grave of his mother and stated that the king desired to harm him. If before the end of the month, his 'business was not settled', he would not come to visit her subsequently. The first of the month drew near and the shaikh's followers became increasingly concerned. The shaikh, however, derived assurance from his submission of the matter to his mother, herself a saintly person, and waited for whatever the future had in store. On the last night before the beginning of the new month, Khusrau Khan rebelled against the sultan and treacherously cut off his head. The issue was thus 'settled'. Nizamuddin Auliya was no longer required to visit the court.

The subsequent rulers never threatened his hospices. The hospices were known for encouraging people to explore the meaning of life, find a way to the Almighty.

Another form of learning, more systematic, and focussed, emanated from the madrasas. During the age of the Tughlaqs, Delhi was known to have a thousand madrasas, most of them had arrangements for lodging and food for students, coming up thereby with some of the early example of residential schools.

Mohammadullah Khalili Qasmi writes in *Madrasa Education*,

> There were as many as one thousand madrasas in Delhi alone during the reign of Sultan Mohammad Tughaq. Salaries for the teachers were fixed from the royal treasury. Education was so common that slave girls used to be Hafiz of the Quran and scholars. Along with religious sciences the rational sciences were also taught.

Incidentally, Firoz Tughlaq was particularly enthusiastic in promoting education. Not just of children from the family of nobles, he wanted children of slaves to attain education too. Besides memorizing the Quran, they were asked to take up rational sciences and learn craft for their livelihood. According to Tarikh Firishta, 180,000 slaves acquired education in science, arts and craft during this period. The Sultan made efforts for imparting education to girls! Hundreds of years before Government of India launched a Beti Bachao, Beti Padhao campaign for life and education of the girl child, Firoz Tughlaq established special madrasas for girls' education. It was a remarkable move considering most nobles even up to 500 years later preferred to invite a scholar home to teach the girls in the privacy of their home. But back then Ibn Batuta found 13 such schools for girls in India! He found hundreds of women in Maharashtra who had memorized the Quran; many among them were slave girls.

Wherever one looked, there was a madrasa in Delhi, each having its own independence in decision-making, charting out the syllabus for the students, etc. Each madrasa concentrated happily on the teaching of the Quran and Hadith to students. But none confined itself to just the transmitted sciences. Each madrasa made an allocation for rational sciences. Thus, mathematics, logic, philosophy, poetry and even Sanskrit were taught. All this without dilution of Persian or Arabic grammar. The subjects taught included Akhlaqiyat (ethics), Ilahiyyat Ilme Hait (astronomy), Intizam-emamlakat (management), Tabiyyat Maashiyyat (economics), Tarikh (history), Falsafa (philosophy) besides Deeniyat (basics of religion). Special attention was paid to fiqh or jurisprudence. The reason was simple: successful madrasa students could look for a job with the royal court if they were familiar with Islamic jurisprudence. Some became qazis, some munsifs, some got into the advisory council of the kings. The Islamic jurisprudence they learnt in madrasas helped in shaping their professional career. They became what in modern parlance can be called as the steel frame of the government. Not that they always fulfilled their responsibilities in conveying the exact Islamic advice for a particular decision of the Sultan. It was not easy either. Many of the Sultans, for instance Ghayasuddin Balban (1266–1287), were clear where their own political jurisdiction took precedence over the shariah. In such a situation, the ulemma did not exactly cover themselves with glory. Adopting a safety-first attitude, they often found ways to agree with the Sultan's decisions, and often (mis) interpreted the shariah accordingly.

That, however, was probably an unavoidable anomaly at a time when the Sultan's word was not just law, but even carried with it the power of life and death. Otherwise, most sultans were generous in their grants to madrasas, and many took great interest in the working and the syllabus of madrasas. Accordingly, they gave great respect and regard to ulemma. India, in early medieval India, was famous in the Islamic world, for its robust scholarship. Not only were there discussions about the Quran and Hadiths, the Hanafi scholars who had come in the trail of the Central Asian hordes, established themselves in India to the extent that most Muslims in India became the followers of the Hanafi sect—it continues to be so in the 21st century. While Hanafi scholars discussed animatedly and often accurately about each of the teachings of Imam Abu Hanifa, it also meant that the madrasas became the centre for the teaching of the Hanafi sect rather than exclusively concentrating on the Quran and Hadith. Unfortunately, none of the Hanafi scholars of India came up with a fresh work to guide the faithful. What they charted out were commentaries on the already published works. In other words, it was like a criticism or appreciation of a published work rather than penning an original work. It had two consequences; first, the Hanafi scholars often found themselves at loggerheads with the khanqahs whose interpretation of Islam was much different; the Hanafis considered music haraam (prohibited) in Islam, the Sufis found in it a way to communion with God. At another level, it meant only the people who had migrated to India from say, Persia or Central Asia, could send their offspring to madrasas. They were the new ashrafs (high caste) who came to monopolize the madrasas, keeping at bay local converts who were initially lower caste Hindus.

Writes Yoginder Sikand in *Bastions of the Believers*, 'Sultan Ghiyasuddin Balban, noted for his fondness for the ulama, followed a strict policy of denying "low" caste origins any post in his administration.' The decision probably stemmed from the writings and advice of well-known historian Ziyauddin Barani who wrote in *Fatwa-e-Jahandari* that the Sultan should make sure that the low caste or ajlaf are denied government services. He is even said to have misinterpreted the Quran to buttress his contention!

In the early years of the advent of Muslims, dissemination of education was a non-formal affair. The rich hired the teachers for the children in their private capacity. Some others learnt at the mosques, still others from the Sufi scholars directly at Sufi dargahs. The earliest madrasa came up in Ajmer in 1191 after the township was captured by Mohammed Ghori, the man whose slave Qutbuddin Aibak later founded the Slave dynasty in 1206, and built the first mosque of North India in the form of Quwwatul Islam Masjid in Delhi. However, before the Ajmer madrasa some sort of small madrasas were set up by scholars who had moved in the wake of the invasion of Mohammed Qasim in Sindh, in 712 AD. Then in Multan there was Madrasa Firozi, built by Nasiruddin Qubacha in the 13th century. Widely respected Sufi Sheikh Bahauddin Zakariyya Multani used to offer his Fajr prayer at this madrasa. Noted scholar of the era Qazi Minhaj Siraj took charge of this madrasa in 1226. He mentions too two other madrasas, Madrasa Mazia and Madrasa Nasiriya; today almost every district of Uttar Pradesh, Bihar, Madhya Pradesh and Telangana has a madrasa by the same name! The Slave dynasty, the Tughlaqs and later the Lodis all contributed to flowering of letters and words. During the time of Sikander Lodi (1489–1517), madrasas were provided new books on rational sciences. However, it was not as if the madrasas were patronized only by the dispensation in Delhi. The kings and sultans in kingdoms of Gujarat, Bidar, Bijapur, Bengal, Jaunpur were all patrons of education. In fact, Jaunpur, in the 15th century, cultivated a reputation for its patronage of arts and sciences as the Shiraz of India. Writes Qasmi,

> The Sharqi Sultans were the rulers of Jaunpur in eastern India. They built hundreds of madrasas. They invited scholars and men of accomplishment from distant countries and granted them valuable fiefs. The building of the madrasa attached to the Atala mosque is extant to this date. Around the mosques sprawls a vast chain of rooms. The famous and clever king of India, Sher Shah Suri had been the alumnus of this every seminary.

Later, Suri as the Sultan saw a madrasa come up under his name (Sher Shahi Madrasa) in Narnol district of Patiala in mid-16th century.

Not far behind was Gujarat. In fact, the Gujarat model paved the way for others. It was the state which saw the advent of the ta'abeen (those who saw and learnt from the companions of the Prophet) and tab-e-ta'abeen (those who learnt from the pupils of the companions). The madrasa system of education flourished in the state under various sultans. Noted Arabic scholar Maulana Abdullah Surati described in his Arabic book *Azwaun ala Tarikh-il Harakat al-Ilmia wa al-Mahadid-il-Islamia wa al-Arabia fi Gujarat* that the state had as many as 32 great institutes of learning in the 15th–16th centuries.

In Bengal too madrasas were the lifeline of the world of scholars. In early 13th century (1212–1227) Ghiyasuddin Awwal ruled over the state. He, as well-known Islamic scholar Muhammad Sajid Qasmi puts it in *Madrasa Education Framework*,

> established madrasas and provided the students with scholarship. Then Ghiyasuddin Sani, along with establishing schools and colleges, founded madrasas in the period of his rule. It is said that he established a college and name it after Madrasa Badi Husain Shah and Nusrat Shah, who were very famous rulers of Bengal. He also constructed many madrasas, schools and colleges. These madrasas and colleges do not exist today, but their remains indicate that they were beautifully constructed and artistically decorated with marbles.

The state kingdoms were conquered by the Great Mughals (1556–1707). While all Mughals were great patrons of art and culture, and none neglected education, the greatest of Mughal rulers, Jalaluddin Akbar (1556–1605) was himself unlettered. Yet he laid stress on education. During his reign, Agra, his capital city, became a centre of knowledge. There was a big madrasa here for which Akbar invited scholars from all over the world. Writes Qasmi,

> It is written that there was a very big madrasa for which Akbar had called an alim from Sheeraz to educate the students. Though the madrasa does not exist today, but a mohalla by the name of Mehellah Madrasa is situated there. Numerous madrasas were established in Fatehpur Sikri. A building was constructed in 1578 for the purpose of religious discussion. Scholars of different schools of thought used to assemble there to have a discussion on varied subjects. Akbar had a deep interest in academic works. Numerous books, related to history, philosophy and religion were written and translated under his supervision. He opened many maktabs and madrasas and provided the students with every facility.

It was during this time that the contents of the madrasa syllabus were changed. As a result, not just Sunni Muslims but also Shias started gaining education in madrasas. Also, non-Muslims joined them in great numbers. For the first time, madrasas started providing education in Vedanta and also Sanskrit for non-Muslim students who may not wish to take special papers on the Quran and Hadith. As a result, non-Muslim students joined in great numbers, aware that a madrasa education opened the portals of employment with the royalty. The reign of Akbar was remarkable for the increasing emphasis laid on rational sciences. Thus, Iranian scholar Mir Fatehullah Shirazi joined his court towards the end of the 16th century. He is said to have been responsible for the introduction of books on astronomy, mathematics, medicine, natural sciences and logic. His pupils diversified to smaller madrasas of the time, taking with them the new stress on rational sciences. Madrasas then were centres of learning of all things beneficial to humanity; from the transmitted knowledge of the Quran and the Hadith (the Hadith education was neglected all along) to the rational approach of mathematics, logic, natural science and medicine. The madrasas also started having pupils from the ajlaf community, thereby acting as a glue within the ummah.

While Jahangir and Shah Jahan are not known to have influenced the system of education, despite their love for learning and the company of scholars, major changes took place during the reign of Aurangzeb Alamgir (1658–1707), himself an accomplished scholar, a man who besides the Quran and Hadith, had read Rumi and Saadi and could compose in Brajbhasa. He was exposed to Persian translations of the Ramayana and the Mahabharata. In a letter to one of his sons, a little before his death, he is said to have remarked, 'I came as a stranger, and I leave as a stranger. My precious life has passed in vain.' Yet Aurangzeb's life was neither in vain nor lacking in impact on the future of madrasas.

The changes made during his time continue to be the spirit of the madrasas, the subsequent additions of modern subjects like physics, biology and geometry notwithstanding. A man wedded to the idea of providing justice, Aurangzeb frequently consulted the ulemma. He is said to have authorized the compilation of the fatwas from the madrasas in the form of a book called Fatwa-e-Alamgiri. It was during his time that Dars-e-Nizami, on which the syllabus of modern madrasas is based, came about. Sikand relates the story,

'Involved in preparing this compendium (Fatwa-e-Alamgiri) of Hanafi law was a renowned alim, Mullah Qutbuddin Sihalwi, a resident of the town of Sihali near Lucknow.... In 1692, he lost his life in a land dispute between his fellow Ansaris and the rival Usmani clan. To compensate for this loss. Aurangzeb offered his sons a mansion that had formerly belonged to a European (firangi) merchant, the Firangi Mahal, in Lucknow. Under Mullah Qutbuddin's third son, Mullah Nizamuddin (d 1748), Firangi Mahal grew into a leading centre of Islamic learning in India.... Mullah Nizamuddin is credited with having prepared a syllabus of studies based on a set of carefully selected texts for the students of Firangi Mahal. Named after him as Dars-e-Nizami, it was heavily skewed in favour of rational sciences, providing students with the sort of education they needed for a job in government services.'

Today, as Sikand states, the syllabi of almost all madrasas in South Asia follow the same basic structure devised by Nizamuddin. Never a rigidly prescribed curriculum, subsequent additions and subtractions have continuously been made. However, the original structure has been left untouched. Incidentally, the original syllabus was pretty taxing for a student, included as it did some 15 books on logic besides others on medicine, engineering, mathematics as also on letter writing and calligraphy. The idea was to produce a well-rounded student who knew something about everything in the world. In all, the syllabus consisted of 79 books!

A scholar of Firangi Mahal madrasa, or a madrasa with a similar syllabus, was almost certain of royal employment. However, things changed a few years after Aurangzeb had passed away. The ulemma had often in the past complained of too much emphasis laid on rational sciences to the detriment of the religious books. However, strong rulers like Akbar and on to Aurangzeb did not brook too much dissent on the subject. After Aurangzeb, the latter Mughals neither enjoyed a long, uninterrupted reign, nor had the power to quash any rebellion. As the Jats, the Marathas and the Sikhs made inroads into the Mughal territory, the ulemma got an opportunity to tell the faithful that only a return to religion would save the community. Led by Shah Waliullah who had at one time gone to Arabia to learn Hadith came back to India and established his madrasa in 1732—some 25 years after Aurangzeb breathed his last. He compiled the six collections of Hadith and did a Persian translation of the Quran. As he preached a dialogue of the four schools of Islamic thought, as opposed to total emphasis on the Hanafi sect, his popularity grew by leaps and bounds. He asked the faithful to adopt the way of life of the Prophet. Critical of rational sciences and Greek philosophy, his growing acceptance meant the madrasas took the first step in dilution of rational sciences from their syllabi. Much worse was to lie in wait the post-First War of Independence for which the British held the Muslims largely responsible. Accordingly, they focussed on madrasas as the centres of scholarly energy. Hundreds of madrasas were destroyed, scores of scholars were hanged to death. The madrasas have not recovered since.

Say, Are those equal, those who and those who do not know? It is those who are endued with understanding that remember (Allah's knowledge).

—VERSE 9, SURAH ZUMAR, THE QURAN

3

THE DEOBAND CONUNDRUM: THE MADRASA THAT STOOD STILL IN TIME

**Dr Rajendra Prasad and Raja Rammohun Roy
Madrasa Aliya**

The summer of 2013 was cruel for the 200-year-old Madrasa Aliya in Rampur. Built by the Nawab family in 1774, the madrasa was demolished in July 2013 following a dispute between the members of madrasa Trust and the local MLA, Samajwadi Party's Azam Khan, now a Lok Sabha MP from Rampur. At its prime, the madrasa was a source of pride for the denizens of the western Uttar Pradesh township, otherwise well known for its Raza Library and notorious for its knives. The madrasa attracted some of the best scholars of Islam in the 20th century, and even the large-scale migration of Muslims to Pakistan following the Partition did not rob the madrasa of its exalted status.

Every year, in the Islamic month of Shabaan, the faithful would gather here to applaud the new graduates, the new hafiz. It was not unusual then for the rectors and academics of the madrasa to tell everybody that once famed social reformer Raja Rammohun Roy studied at Madrasa Aliya. When, how or where was never discussed. The assembled parents, keen to bask in the reflected glory, never asked, if it was the madrasa in Rampur or the one in Bengal where Roy studied. Of course, the old-timers knew that Roy had not studied in Rampur, but the very fact that he had spent a little time studying in a madrasa by the name of Aliya provided reason to gloat over. No cross-questions popped up. The Muslims of Rampur were not alone in soaking in the moment. The local Hindus, the Pandits joined them too. Those were days of a shared past, and Madrasa Aliya stood as a shining example. It was heart-warming to see the maulvis ask the youngsters to learn Arabic the way Roy did, and to rise in life the way he did. The inspiration for the talib-e-ilm (students) came not from West Asian history or a conqueror but from some of the biggest social reformers and freedom fighters of India.

As for Roy, well, he studied in a madrasa in Bengal, probably called Madrasa Aliya too, but gained actual mastery of Persian and Arabic at Madrasa Mujibia in Phulwari Sharif in Patna. When Roy came to Madrasa Mujibia, he was not more than 12, but had already learnt elementary Persian under a maulvi back home in Bengal. At Madrasa Mujibia, Roy mastered Arabic to the extent that he could read the Quran in the Arabic original without any maulvi's help. Though he preached monotheism, Roy did not confine himself to the study of Islam, or the Quran. At the madrasa he studied the works of medieval Sufis, and apprised himself with the Arabic translations of the works of Aristotle and Plato. While these accomplishments show Roy to be a multifaceted genius that he was, they also tell us that the madrasas in pre-Independence India were not the monopoly of Muslims, or mere centres to learn to read the Quran. The subjects they taught were as vast as the range of their students. Besides the Quran and Hadiths, they taught Fiqh as also mathematics, poetry, physics, geography and the like. Each day, each year came laced with possibilities of fresh learning. They counted among the students, the richest of people, the heirs of nawabs, the sons of the best-read Brahmins, etc. The madrasas then were a place where the best of pluralist India gathered to learn. Rare was a Hindu family in the vicinity of a madrasa that did not send its son for learning. Most came for primary learning at the maktab, many stayed on for higher learning at the madrasa. Little wonder, the officials at Madrasa Aliya could not desist from claiming credit for Roy's learning!

It was the same ethos of the madrasas that drew Rajendra Prasad to them in the early years of his life. Later, to be the first President of India, Dr Rajendra Prasad too learnt under a maulvi in his childhood. With education being independent of teachers' personal faith, many of our early politicians went to madrasas and maulvis.

Writes Dr Rajendra Prasad in his autobiography (*Autobiography:; Rajendra Prasad*)

> I began schooling when I was five of six, along with two of my cousins, the elder of whom was Jamuna Prasad, our leader in games and boyish pranks. According to custom, a Maulvi Saheb had to initiate us into the alphabet. On the first day he began our education in the name of Allah and an offering was made to him. Sweets were then distributed all around.

Incidentally, to this day, many Muslims begin the education of their children at the age of four with a small ceremony called Bismillah– In the name of Allah. On this day, the child is taught his first alphabets and sweets are distributed to family and friends. Much like it was with Dr Rajendra Prasad when he was initiated.

The former President recalls in his autobiography,

> Our study of Persian, meanwhile, progressed. In six months, we picked up the Persian alphabet and started reading the Karima. Then the Maulvi Saheb left us. Another Maulvi was appointed. He was a serious-minded man and a good teacher. He taught us for two years and we completed the Karima, Mamkima, Khushahal Simiya, Dastur-il-Simiya, Gulistan, Bostan, etc. Thursday afternoons and Fridays were holidays for us and during those days we learnt counting, and picked up the Kaithi script. The Maulvi lived in a room in the house adjoining ours. The maktab (school) was located in a verandah of his house. We would sit on a takht-posh (wooden cot) and the Maulvi on his own. The school began early in the morning. We had to repeat the previous day's lesson which we had learnt by heart. After we had finished, we passed on to the next lesson.... We would also practise writing on a wooden plank.... After sunset, we would begin again and study in the light of an oil lamp. When the Maulvi gave us leave, we would bow reverentially and go home.

It was the same abiding respect that came to the fore years later when as the President of India, Dr Rajendra Prasad visited Darul

'Ulum, Deoband, probably the best-known Islamic seminary in the country. Addressing the students and their ustad at the madrasa, he said,

> I have been hearing about the Darul 'Ulum for a long time now, and have, ever since I first heard of it, wanted to come here, and today that wish has been fulfilled. The elders of the Darul 'Ulum acquired and imparted knowledge for its own sake. There have been few people in the past that did this, and they were even more respected than the kings. Today, the elders of the Darul 'Ulum are walking in this path, and I believe that this is a service not only to the Darul 'Ulum itself, nor only of the Muslims alone, but in fact, of the entire country, and indeed of the whole world.

Interestingly, while the madrasas recall the student days of Dr Rajendra Prasad and Ram Rammohun Roy, they are not as enthusiastic talking about ace Urdu writer Munshi Premchand, who too, at the age of seven, enrolled in a madrasa in Lalpur near Banaras, and learnt Urdu and Persian from the maulvi there. Never mind. Their relative silence on the illustrious writer does nothing to take away from the fact that madrasas in 19th and early 20th centuries were seminaries of complete learning where pupils of all faiths gathered. Their syllabus went beyond religion to the realm of languages, sciences, mathematics, philosophy and poetry. Very much similar to their counterparts in Samarkand, they were, in some ways, the precursors of the modern-day missionary schools. They gave India its first President, and our society some of the biggest social reformers and writers.

. . .

Terrorism in the true sense of the word is an aggressive act against innocent persons, without legitimacy. The aim is to frighten them. Acts of similar type may be committed by individual, group, nation or the country that may be classified as terrorist activity, if the aim is to terrorize the common person or the opponent for achieving certain ends.

That type of terrorism has no place in Islamic Shariah. The Holy Quran makes it explicit that killing an innocent person is equivalent to killing the whole humankind.

A verse in Surah Maidah states,

> If anyone slew a person unless it be for murder or for spreading mischief in the land it would be as If he slew the whole people: and if anyone saved a life. It would be as if he saved the life of the whole people.[1] (Al-Maidah. verse 32)

The failure of the First War of Independence in 1857 had a devastating impact. While the country lost an opportunity to throw off the imperial yoke, the Muslim community in particular had to bear the brunt of the British excesses. Hundreds of Islamic clerics were executed, scores of mosques were defiled and madrasas unceremoniously shut down. Clearly, the British regarded Muslims as their arch enemies. The attack on a masjid or a madrasa was as much an attack on India as a community's symbols of pride. While a historic mosque like Fatehpuri Masjid in Delhi lapsed into the hands of a local trader, the Jama Masjid and Ghata Masjid fell into the hands of the imperial forces. Their horses were anchored here, a bakery flourished too. During the war, some of the ulemma had waged an open struggle against the British. Thana Bhawan, in modern Uttar Pradesh, was the site of rebellion against the British. The Islamic clerics took on the British in huge numbers here. Noted scholar Farhat Tabassum referred to their contribution in the book *Deoband Ulema's Movement for the Freedom of India* (Manak),

> The first phase of the battle started with an attack on British soldiers who were passing along the Bagh-e-Sher Ali Road. A British soldier was killed and Indians managed to seize some weapons, including a cannon. The attack from Bagh-e-Sher Ali was a successful attempt of the revolutionaries

---

[1] http://www.darululoom-deoband.com/english

against the British. When the news of the British attack from Saharanpur reached the revolutionaries, they became worried, as they had no advanced weapons. The revolutionaries decided to seize the weapons from the British. A plan was worked out to attack British troops passing by Bagh-e-Sher Ali Road. The garden along the road proved very helpful as a place of hiding for the revolutionaries. Haji Imdadullah led a battalion of 30–40 revolutionaries. All of them hid themselves in the garden and when the British soldiers were passing through the road, they pounced on them. One British soldier was killed. The attack was very successful from the point of view of the Indian revolutionaries as they managed to seize some weapons and a powerful cannon.

The British, inevitably, did not take it lying down. The British forces surrounded Thana Bhavan. Also reports came in that they had laid siege to Shamli, and the revolutionaries rushed there. Hiding in a mosque, they attacked the British forces. It was in this battle that Maulana Qasim Nanautavi played a prominent role. With him were the likes of Maulana Imam Rabbani, Maulana Rashid Ahmed and Maulana Hafeez, later to be involved in the dissemination of education among the faithful.

They fought the British army tooth and nail in Shamli. Haji Imdadullah was the commander-in-chief of the rebel forces. Maulana Mohammed Qasim Nanautawi, Maulana Rasheed Ahmad Gangohi and Hafiz Zamin Shaheed acted as wing commanders. The British quelled the rebellion with a heavy hand. Imdadullah escaped to Makkah. Zamin Shaheed was martyred, Gangohi was captured, put on trial and later freed. Nanautavi went into hiding. He came back a few years later to spearhead the movement for the foundation of Darul Uloom Deoband, an institution that would prepare scholars to guide the community. It came about at a time when any surviving madrasa could no longer hope for imperial grants as was the case during the time of the Mughals. With the community living in a state of fear and rising economic challenges, the odds were stacked up against madrasas. They had to find ways to sustain themselves, or rely on a handful of community members who might still have disposable resources. At this time, Maulana Nanautavi led the movement for the revival of pristine Islam. The idea was to make every Muslim well versed with the Quran and Hadith, thereby empowering him. He wanted the younger generation to know Islam well before going on to learn secular subjects. With this aim in mind, he reduced the period of study at a madrasa from 10 to 6 years. Thus, a boy who joined before the age of 9–10, could hope to be an alim by the age of 15, and then proceed for secular learning. This, however, was the first step towards bifurcation of education in modern India.

Students coming out of the seminary after classes

Though technically a madrasa, Deoband was supposed to give the community its identity back, and help in restoration of its lost pride. In fact, Maulana Mahmood Hasan, the first student here, never ever considered it just a madrasa. Once, he is reported to have said, 'Did Maulana (Nanautavi) build this madrasa just to learn and teach? The madrasa was established before my eyes. As I know the institution was established after the defeat of 1857 to prepare some people to recover the loss of 1857.' Interestingly, the first teacher of Deoband as also the first student, were both called Mahmood, the former being called Mullah Mahmood, the latter answering to Mahmood Hasan.

A view of the historic building

Incidentally, the Deoband seminary was set up not only to provide quality religious education, but also as a counter to Lord Macaulay's education system. As Mufti Shafi Usman is quoted by Muhammadullah Khalili Qasmi in *Madrasa Education* (Manak),

The key purpose of Darul Uloom was to foil the attempts made by Lord Macaulay's education and to produce a bunch of gallant ulamma who not only can perform the duty of saving religion in its true form but can also deliver it to the succeeding generations. So that any time when Muslims can get freedom from colonial rule they can find the Islamic teachings in true and original form.

Thus a self-financed seminary Darul Uloom, Deoband came into existence in 1866, and a community licking its wounds post 1857 took recourse to faith to move ahead. The past was all about imperial patronage. The future was going to be about building private institutions with personal money. And madrasas had to depend on private donations to meet their expenses. Realizing the possibility of Deoband spawning off other madrasas, Nanautavi laid down eight principles for the new seminary: The madrasa men should look for ways to increase donation, provide food to students so that they do not leave to earn a living, the interests of the madrasa should be paramount and the rector should consult the advisory board on key issues, the madrasa teachers should not nurse a big ego, teaching material provided for the year should be completed, the madrasas should be careful about the donors, and their source of income, the share of the government and the rich seems dangerous, and the donations of those who do not wish name and fame are blissful.

Nanautavi's views of Deoband being a role model for other small madrasas proved correct. Today, thousands of madrasas across India follow the Deoband model. Incidentally, the site was chosen because Maulana Rafiuddin saw the Kabah in the garden of Deoband in a dream. It was this dream which inspired Nanautavi to start Darul Uloom in Deoband. The madrasa started in interesting circumstances. It was Friday, 30 May 1857, when the madrasa was founded under a pomegranate tree in Masjid-e-Chatta. Maulana Mahmood Hasan was the first student, and Mullah Mehmood the first teacher. Then it became an institution some nine years later. The new institution chose to follow the Dars-i-Nizami pattern with a few alterations. While it concentrated on the Quran and Hadith, certain time-worn books, like those on Aristotelian philosophy and logic, were cast aside. And a few secular ones added by and by. But at its core, the Deobandi mode

A niche of history: Darul Uloom, Deoband in 1950

of education concentrated on transmitted sciences and fiqh. Unfortunately, the animosity of the British towards the Muslims, and their patronage of rational sciences meant Deoband scholars had to tread with caution in the world of science. As Deobandis opposed the British, it also meant a silent opposition to matters of science. This theory of enemy's friend (science) being an enemy was to cost the community dear. What if the alims could distinguish between being opponents of the British, not necessarily all their knowledge? What if Deoband had followed matters of science and technology, mathematics and computers, English and Hindi with the same zest it exhibited in training scholars of

Islam? And had spoken out as vehemently about the association of terrorism with Islam?

A prayer in progress

Darul Uloom Nadwatul Ulamma, Lucknow

New Delhi Jama Masjid is a rare mosque in the Capital. In fact, it is among a handful in the entire country. While a vast majority of mosques in North India have a brief talk or discussion after Fajr (dawn) and Asar prayers on Fazail-e-Amaal, Tablighi Jamaat's book of Hadiths and anecdotes, New Delhi Jama Masjid has no space for discussion on a book that combines authentic and inauthentic Hadiths. The masjid concentrates on the Quran. While the mosque does not register a significant footfall in Fajr prayers as it is located in an area full of government offices, it attracts a fair number of worshippers in its Zuhr prayers every afternoon. It is also the time, the imam follows the prayer with a brief discussion on some verses from the Quran. There have been times when the mosque has held special lectures on learning Quranic Arabic too. All this is in contrast to what happens at most mosques. Incidentally, the imam is well versed with English and Arabic. There have been occasions when visiting dignitaries from Saudi Arabia have addressed the faithful here in Arabic, and the imam has happily played a translator. On other occasions, when the congregation has included people from Malaysia, Palestine, South Africa and other countries, the imam has used English besides Urdu as part of his address, so that everybody could follow it, or at least, understand the spirit of the address. It is way different from what happens at most mosques where even the Friday khutba is not always translated into the local language by the imam—this is a world removed from what happens at the Prophet's mosque in Madina where the Friday khutba is translated into major languages like English, Urdu, Turkish and even French.

The reason is simple. The imam of the mosque is a product of Darul Uloom Nadwatul Ulama in Lucknow. It is a body which concentrates on the Quran and imparts knowledge of Arabic to its students. Nadwa includes both classical and modern Arabic in its syllabus. The seminary also excludes some of the medieval sciences that have lost their relevance. Also cast aside have been many scholastic sciences and philosophical debates as they ceased to have any relevance in modern-day. Today, Nadwa offers all-encompassing education, ranging from the primary to the university stage in the theological branches of learning and Arabic literature. From the primary to clearing the university-level exams, it takes a student about 16 years. At the primary level, which is of six years, a student is imparted elementary knowledge of English, Hindi and Urdu as well as general sciences, mathematics and social sciences, etc. Grammar of Persian as also Arabic is taught at the secondary level. The higher secondary is reserved for instruction in English, Arabic and Persian besides Islamic history. Then the students who opt for alimiyat have to study Islamic jurisprudence, tafseer and Hadith.

The body's present is rooted in its past. Nadwatul Ulamma was started in 1894 in response to the activities of Christian missionaries and the overpowering desire to embrace the West. With the promotion of knowledge of science, and coming about of secularism, a need was felt for an Islamic seminary that will not stay away from science and, at the same time, be true to its Islamic foundations. Thus, Nadwatul Uloom was founded as a bridge between Aligarh Muslim University (AMU) with its overweening emphasis on science and Darul Uloom, Deoband with its grudging acceptance of the same. At the forefront of the movement was Maulana Mohammed Ali Mungeri who was a strong advocate of bringing together Islam and modern education:[2]

> There is a great need for a group of ulemma which should also be in touch with the current affairs and developments. It should know what the rules of governance are and what type of relations should it have with the government. Against such a background he decided to establish a madrasa which would impart religious as well as scientific education. Incidentally, one aim of the body was to iron out the differences between the ulemma and unite them for the cause of Islam. When a teacher of madrasa Islamia, Faizabad, Maulana Mushtaq Ali Nageenavi, was sent on a tour of important places of the country in the early years of the body's foundation, he was given a letter by the first rector of the Nadwatul Ulamma listing its objectives.

> At present, differences among the ulemma is a cause of a great loss to the community. Ulemma have differences on petty issues. Because of this, the image of both the ulemma and Islam is being tarnished in the eyes of the people. This body will ensure that no difference or conflict arises and, if at all it does, it will sort it out amicably.

---

[2] https://attahawi.files.wordpress.com/2009/07/deoband-ulamas-movement.pdf

Though the body failed in its avowed purpose of bringing the intellectuals together—at its second convention, one of its patrons, Maulana Shibli Nomani bemoaned the indifferent attitude of the ulemma and their petty squabbles—it did succeed in making the common Muslims aware of the need to converge the old learning with the new. And when newer madrasas like Madrasatul Asla were established in Azamgarh, it marked a little triumph for the ideology of Nadwatul Uloom. The new madrasa laid emphasis on understanding the Quran and knowledge of Arabic. Soon, it was joined by Jamiyatul Falah in Azamgarh. It too aimed to produce scholars of the Quran and Sunnah who would be well versed in non-Islamic issues too. Around the same time, Jamiya Dar-us-Salaam came up in Omerabad. Called the Nadwa of the South, Dar-us-Salaam promoted a composite society. It too laid emphasis on the Quran and the knowledge of Arabic. Shunning bifurcation, the ideal here was all about assimilation.

Just like the imam at the New Delhi Jama Masjid does. Wonder what will be repercussions if more imams were to follow suit? Maybe, the Quran and its message would build a home with everybody. And, in turn, science, mathematics, logic, etc., would be promoted. After all, the Quran asks us to reason, to explore.

Knowledge is the life of Islam, and the pillar of faith

—PROPHET MUHAMMAD (PBUH)

MADRASAS IN MODERN INDIA: SORRY STATE, LOFTY PRINCIPLES?

Abdul Qayyum
Madrasa Husain Bux, Delhi

Back in the 1960s and 1970s, a story went that the Madrasa Husain Bux was home to all. There was Yaqub tea stall at the main gate of the madrasa. At the wicket gate on a worn-out coir cot rested an old woman Neelam, too weak to sit except when the muezzin called for prayer from inside the madrasa. Out of deference, and with much effort, she managed to raise her body to rest on her elbows. Then Neelam with her son Bishan and daughter-in-law Chhaya would sit together on their cot in absolute silence. The noise from Yaqub tea stall too died down for a few minutes, his constant admonition of his attendant broken by the muezzin's call. Once the azaan was over, din resumed at the tea stall, and Neelam too went back to her usual reclining position.

That was outside the madrasa. Inside it, the story went, the jinns dwelled. Almost everybody you met had a jinn story to reveal. They were not kind to anybody who missed a prayer, went one story. It was easily superseded by another, according to which the imam's wife had her bed turned upside down at the time of Fajr (dawn) prayers because she did not get up to offer her prayers. The best was, of course, the one that talked of a boy who had his neck twisted because he had attended to nature's call while standing in the urinal. How many of them were true or just gained traction through gossip nobody would know. The effect of the stories ensured that no worshipper used the corridor of the madrasa where the jinns were said to dwell. The corridor had no window, no light. It emitted the kind of smell found in dank, dingy and desultory monuments. The madrasa too was not much short of a monument. Built in 1852, freedom fighters would often gather here for planning the strategy for the days ahead in the early 20th century. Often, most of them used to go to Sharif Manzil in Ballimaran, not far from the famous Chandni Chowk. But whenever the gathering got too big, they would assemble at the madrasa, knowing its courtyard had ample space for them all. The madrasa was also a little removed from the prying eyes of the British who had reduced the historic Jama Masjid to a horse stable after the First War of Independence, and the neighbouring Ghata Masjid to a bakery. Madrasa Husain Bux, located a few brisk steps from Jama Masjid, survived. It was helped, of course, by the fact that the lane leading to the madrasa was closed to any vehicular traffic except a cycle or a scooter

Till the time of the Independence, the madrasa did not use a loudspeaker for the daily azaan. It changed some time in the late 1950s when the faithful would be reminded to pray through the muezzin's invitation extended over a microphone. Until the late 1960s, the madrasa desisted from hiring a muezzin for the purpose of maintenance of the premises and pronouncement of the azaan. The locals happily took turn to call the faithful for prayer. Sometime in the mid-1960s though, a gentleman from Bihar who had attended a madrasa in Pureni and could be said to have at least elementary knowledge of Islam joined as the muezzin. The going for Abdul Qayyum was not easy. The madrasa, in contrast to most others in the Walled City of Delhi, was a big one. More than 50 men could stand shoulder to shoulder in prayer at the same time. The biggish courtyard had rooms all around, and wings to its northern and southern ends. Then there were some more rooms on the first floor. Cleaning all the rooms, the courtyard, the corridors and the prayer hall was a tough ask. And then to be expected to maintain the prayer timings by the minute! Abdul Qayyum did it all with sincerity, putting up a gritty resistance whenever somebody tried to find a replacement. Gradually, the muezzin became an integral part of the madrasa, and even the younger imams started taking his counsel. He saw generations of talib-e-ilm (students) come, learn and leave. Many went back to their small towns in Uttar Pradesh and Bihar; one or two fortunate ones went to Deoband to pursue higher studies. A couple of them even went to Canada and England! Whenever they returned, which was not more often than once in a couple of years, they were feted; their counsel on any subject immediately respected.

Abdul Qayyum, a muezzin at the historic
Madrasa Hussain Bux for the past 50 years

On the personal front, Abdul Qayyum got married, and was blessed with four sons. His desire to have a daughter drove him on until he was blessed with two daughters in succession. He stayed in the one-room tenement on the first floor of the madrasa with his wife and brood. As his family grew, he supplemented his meagre earnings from the madrasa by setting up a stall near Jama Masjid. He sold prayer mats there. It helped him pay for the school fees of two of his sons.

The madrasa too grew from strength to strength, building on from a mere maktab (primary school) in the initial days to one offering certificates and degrees equivalent to high school and graduation. The students came from far and near, some from Andhra Pradesh and Maharashtra, most from Uttar Pradesh and Bihar. The madrasa proved ahead of its times. Back in the 1970s when nobody provided rugs and carpets to students, the madrasa lined its classrooms with wall to wall carpets and rugs. For day scholars, there were durries. Professionalism came by the way classes were announced through a bell. The students hunched over a wooden bench, poring over the sacred text from around 8 in the morning to noon. After a break for afternoon prayer and lunch, they would be back in class. This time to learn Persian, Arabic, even tajveed and fiqh—deriving the root words, and understanding Islamic jurisprudence. It went on till the muezzin called everybody for Asar prayers a little more than an hour before sunset.

As for the muezzin, he never asked any of his six children to study at Madrasa Husain Bux. All that he made sure was each child could learn to recite the Quran at the madrasa. Once that was done, each of the kids was sent to a local primary or secondary school. Every afternoon, as the devotees trickled out after Zuhr prayers, the muezzin's kids would be entering the mosque in their school uniform, shirt, pants, tie and all. Their western attire would invite quizzical looks and criticism. Some wondered aloud if the muezzin had gone astray. Abdul Qayyum though kept his head bowed, and lips silent. He had a goal in mind: It was English medium of instruction that he sought for his children. He wanted them to be able to read the Quran. He wanted that they should be able to speak in English, pick up jobs outside and not stay confined to a madrasa. Against steep odds, he sent his grown-up children to Delhi University and Jamia Millia Islamia University. He was not done though. His youngest daughter was to go on to do her PhD from Delhi University, undoubtedly making her unlettered mother, who had had to sell household utility items to manage her fees, proud. As for the muezzin, it was a mission accomplished. He spent his entire life in Madrasa Husain Bux, but knew there was life beyond the madrasa.

Abdul Qayyum still lives and works at the madrasa. Most of his children have moved out. Not so the PhD scholar. The madrasa continues to provide the ground under her feet, and a roof over her head. Time to take on the world.

. . .

For every regular madrasa with its affiliation in place, its structure clearly authorized, its syllabus clearly marked, there are scores of irregular, not illegal madrasas operating across the length and breadth of the country. As you drive on the highway, it is not uncommon to come across a simple structure by the side of green fields. Its main wall would be whitewashed, its door, or at times, its dome would be in green. More often than not, it would be a madrasa! Children from nearby villages would come here to get Islamic education. The madrasas would be manned by a couple of persons only. Not often will it have even basic facilities to offer its students. Usually, there is an electricity connection but no guarantee of uninterrupted power supply. Something like an inverter is hardly ever used. At times, as in madrasas in Maharashtra, Karnataka and Andhra Pradesh, it will have a water pipeline for ablution purposes. At others, a simple hand-pump meets all requirements of water, as in large tracts of Uttar Pradesh and Bihar. These madrasas, which offer elementary Islamic learning in the form of hifz facilities, are run on community funding. There is no financial support from any madrasa board or any of the bigger madrasas whose syllabus they usually follow. With a strength of 50–300 students, these madrasas follow the Deoband template. Only occasionally, a Jamaat-e-Islami principle is followed. Though some of them have started helping their students to pursue secular learning alongside memorization sessions of the Quran, most do not simply because their students are first-generation learners, and hail form extremely poor families. The families cannot afford to buy books for class X matriculation examinations or even to pay the fee. They are thus happy if their child passes out of a madrasa as a hafiz. No expenditure is involved in becoming a hafiz-e-Quran, and the families are content. The newly minted hafiz can hope to augment the family's income by taking up a job as an imam in a mosque in the vicinity.

Interestingly, though they operate informally, the madrasas have a well-etched-out network of fund collection, they send their safir or representative to mosques in the region, preferring those with a higher footfall. The safir, in turn, comes towards the evening when most people would have come back from work, and will be in a position to help out with a token donation. Most of these madrasas have their receipt books in place for any such transaction; for example, Madrasa Raah-e-Najat in Delhi's Sundar Nagari. The 26-year-old madrasa has a valid bank account and is happy to share its address and IFSC code on its receipt book. Not as evolved or upright is a madrasa in Aashta in Sehrore district of Madhya Pradesh. The small madrasa with around 70 students, including 40 day scholars, operates under a local Jama Masjid. The madrasa has no water connection, drawing water from a borewell nearby. The locals do not even recall its name; most just address it as 'masjid wala madrasa'. Such are the vagaries of India's largest informal sector centres of learning. Very little by way of history, even less by way of incentive to meritorious students, yet these madrasas play a crucial role: their students can neither afford any other education, or even madrasa education elsewhere, nor do they lay much stock by the madrasa's registration or the lack of it. A simple acknowledgement of their skills at a so-called graduation ceremony two weeks before Ramadan gets them the social approval they seek. The madrasas are content too, built as they usually are, on a piece of land donated by a Good Samaritan. Like their students, the aspirations of the madrasas and their management are extremely limited too. Satisfied are they with rolling out hafiz-e-Quran every year. Those wishing to be engineers, doctors, accountants or journalists can enrol elsewhere. The small, irregular but teeming madrasas are happy that the youngsters who otherwise would have wasted their time watching movies, or indulging in anti-social activities, get basic knowledge of Islam and can hope to live a righteous life.

Madrasa Maqsood Ashrafiya, Village Mujahid Khani, Amethi

All around Madrasa Maqsood Ashrafiya, life moves serenely. The quiet in the air can almost be heard. All through the year, the farmers are busy, now sowing wheat, now harvesting it. Now sowing rice, now harvesting it. Some have tractors for their fields; many still use bullocks. The means of transport are elementary; some have a cycle, most use tempo, a popular public transport vehicle in rural areas. Not every child is enrolled in schools. Amidst a swirl of bees during daytime and mosquitoes in the evening, village Mujahid Khani maintains its peace.

However, there is one small place in the village which has not known lasting peace for the past decade, or maybe a bit more. It is the village madrasa. Called, rather loftily, Madrasa Maqsood Ashrafiya, the madrasa struggles for consistency. No teacher who is appointed here lasts long enough to make a difference to the lives of its 50 students or so. While in metropolises, teachers often move from one institution to another as part of upward mobility in career, here the challenges are existential. The maulanas are appointed for merely ₹5,000 per month. This amount has to come from the local villagers as the elementary madrasa is not registered. The villagers, in turn, are dependent on the erratic earnings from their farms. If it rains well, and there is a good crop, the maulana in the madrasa can hope to get his salary on time. If the crop fails, the maulana's pocket is impacted too. Not many can bear these erratic ways. Most move out after a few months. Then a fresh search starts to find a solitary teacher to teach students from the age of 6 to 17–18! Another young man joins. He too meets the same fate.

Meanwhile, the students at the madrasa continue their search to learn to recite the Quran, pick up elementary Arabic or to do hifz. The hifz students suffer the most. When a maulana joins the madrasa, in the name of revision, he often starts afresh from the first chapter. Thus, a student who could have memorized the Quran in three years ends up taking up to five years. This in turn sets his family back. The family is often hopeful of the boy becoming a hafiz soon in order to pick up a job as an imam somewhere, and help in the family's earnings. It is a vicious circle at the madrasa. The local families cannot pay the imam or the maulanas on time, their own children's education is delayed. Accordingly, their hunt for a job is postponed.

Incidentally, the madrasa which has been in existence for more than a decade, to this date, has only two rooms with a proper ceiling. The students sit here cross-legged on the floor as they place a copy of the Quran on the bench and try to memorize it verse by verse. It is a long haul, made more challenging by the enervating heat, sapping humidity and constantly buzzing bees. Yet, the two rooms are the best place to be in at the madrasa. Rest of the space in the 150-yard plot does not have concrete flooring either. The electric supply at the premises is erratic at best, the water supply non-existent. The age-old hand-pump is the sole reliable companion, be it quenching the students' thirst, or the pious doing the ablution before a prayer. During rains, it gets difficult for students to reach their classrooms. They have to top-toe across all the squelch and squalor. At the height of winters, the madrasa perforce has to open late. More often than not, it is dependent on natural light and air. Hence, it becomes impossible to start lessons in winters immediately after dawn prayers.

At Madrasa Maqsood Ashrafiya, life is neither smooth nor serene. Every day is a challenge for the teacher and the taught. So unlike the village in which it stands as a sad reminder of the tragic state of some of our Islamic learning centres. And to think these penury-struck places of learning are dubbed as dens of terrorism by the ignorant and the irresponsible!

Jamia Mahad-e-Noor, Qidwai Nagar, Dadri

'For the past 10 years, we have survived on donations of the pious. Most people who come here, or who live in the neighbourhood, are poor. They give ₹1 or ₹2 in donation. Some well off people give ₹50 or ₹100, but even that amount is not sufficient. We get zero help from the State or any bigger institution. Despite the locals' help, the madrasa is still just a physical structure. We have an area of 1,400 feet, but due to paucity of funds, it is difficult to complete the madrasa. We have around 250 students here, including about 25 hostellers. However, we are not able to give any facilities to our hostellers. So many leave midway. There is very little we can do to retain them as there is just not enough money. Remember, we have four teachers, who too have to be paid. Their salary is around ₹5,000. In one case it goes up to ₹8,000. From the donations of ₹1 or ₹2, we have to run the entire madrasa. We cannot charge the students as they come from poor background. They have to be given the books too. We have some girls too who come to study. They sit separately from the guys. All of them are in pre-puberty years. There is a dedicated teacher for them. But, be it boys or girls, we avoid corporal punishment though we have learnt from our ustad through punishment. I am determined that the relationship between the teacher and the student should one be of love and respect. It takes time for the relationship to evolve, but if it does, it stays true for a lifetime. If you cane the student, he will never respect you, though he might fear you.'

These are the words of Abdus Sattar Qasmi, the sole man incharge of Madrasa Jamia Mahad-e-Noor in Dadri. The madrasa is located barely 3 kilometres from the place where the unfortunate Akhlaq was lynched in September 2015. 'Things have never been the same since then. That is the reason, I ask the teachers not to be too strict with the students. If anything wrong takes place, there are forces which will try to force the government to close down the madrasas in the name of alleged torture of students. We have to be careful.'

Mahad-e-Noor in Dadri is one of the madrasas
struggling due to a paucity of funds

The madrasa is not recognized yet though Qasmi claims their application is pending for recognition with the state Madrasa Board as also the Allahabad Board.

Qasmi, whose current goal is to have a water pipeline for the madrasa, says, 'We prepare our students to be maulvi and hafiz. We also teach tajweed and offer a three-year alim course. We want to add science, maths, English also, but we have to do things gradually. The locals will have to be prepared for this. Most are uneducated. If we add all the subject immediately, they might think we have gone astray. In Ramadan, it gets difficult. More people come here. For ablution, we used a hand-pump. But in Ramadan, there are more people who come for prayer. So we keep a big drum filled with water. That is used for ablution. I am waiting for the day we will have proper pipelines and water in taps'.

Mahad-e-Noor: Celebrating Republic Day every year where both boys and girls participate with enthusiasm

The madrasa, still some way from completion, however, marks the fulfilment of a long journey for Qasmi. Back in 1990, he had enrolled to become a doctor with AMU. Unfortunately, there was violence on the campus and the university was closed sine die.

'Our financial condition was not very sound. I waited for some time for the university to be re-opened. Meanwhile, a local man whom I knew, took me to Hardwaganj where I taught students for three months. As the university was still to re-open, I continued teaching. Finally, I did my MA in Urdu. Earlier, I have studied in Deoband. Life has not been easy. When I joined AMU I did not visualize it will shape up this way. Today, I have meagre earnings from the madrasa. I am almost fully dependent on money from farming in Hapur. That money too is limited. As a result, I do not know how to pay the coaching fee of my younger son who plans to take the NEET exam next year. My elder son is in BA Final. I have some more work to do before I can pass on the baton to them. It is difficult, but I am glad I could get college education for my children. With madrasa education, they could not have hoped to land a job. The times we are living in are sensitive. People in the government look at madrasas with an eye of suspicion. I do not know for how long can the madrasas continue, but they play an important role to teach the children of poor families. At the very minimum, they help the government to spread literacy. They should be given credit for that.'

Jamia Naseeriya Islamia Near Kunwewali Masjid, Behta Hajipur, Loni border, Ghaziabad

If you drive from Ghaziabad towards Delhi, you are quite likely to come across plenty of brick-lined structures. Not many would have a coast of cement to cover the walls from outside. The walls have a layer of cement on the inside. Every penny has to be saved, so the outside is stark. Amidst blaring horns of bikes and cars, there will be a jingle of cycle and rickshaw bells too. Every other corner will have posters of the Hindi films playing at a local cinema. The films here usually arrive late, much after gracing the halls at prime halls of New Delhi. Occasionally, a Sunny Deol or a Salman Khan film would open alongside Delhi. Then there is a constant clank of bells and blaring horns. It seems Loni loves its cinema.

Ironically, what it also loves are its mosques and madrasas. Usually painted a garish green to go with whitewashed walls, not many are distinct enough from a distance. Most are modest, and easily lost in the vast expanse of semi-complete buildings. The best way to make out a masjid or a madrasa is the sight of pre-teen and teenage boys dressed in crisp kurta–pyjama and a skullcap running around with a copy of one of the chapters of the Quran. Or at times, just a white takhti, a wooden board on which they learn to write with a neat hand. That is how they told the boys in the 1960s and 1970s. That is how they still teach them here in 2019.

Amidst it all stands the 15-year-old Madrasa Jamia Naseeriya Islamia. If the name is a mouthful, the madrasa itself is in a sorry state, begging for funds and urgent attention. It started in 2004 but the building is yet to be completed. An acute dearth of funds means it is not likely to have a fresh round of cement or paint anytime soon. The flooring across this 175-metre plot is yet to be completed. While the main room and the courtyard leading to it have cemented flooring, rest all is covered with bricks laid down in a criss-cross pattern. In local language, they call it kharanja. In monsoon, water seeps through leaving a squelching sound at every step. In summers, it gets unbearably hot.

At the madrasa, one finds some 30 students are hostellers. They sleep in one section of the room which they use for their studies during daytime. No separate room, no privacy, no beds, no curtains. Just a rug under their body, not much else. The pillows, if any, are brought by the students themselves, as are other essential items. Bad as their condition is, the hall proper where the prayers are held is not much better. The cement on the floor is broken at several places, the wooden benches are in need of repair too.

The madrasa also attracts day scholars, some 40 of them from the neighbourhood. Nearly all of them are from economically enfeebled families. The families cannot afford to send them to a regular school with a monthly fee of ₹100–₹150. The madrasa that provides free religious education seems an attractive option to them. To teach these 70-odd students, there are two teachers on a salary of ₹8,000 each. A cook prepares the food for the hostellers. Then there is the incharge Mohammed Ismail. All the expenses of the madrasa, amounting to ₹40,000 every month, are borne through local charity. Some kind-hearted people give it ₹10 a month, others ₹100. Only rarely does a generous soul part with ₹1,000 every month. While some amount is locally collected, a lot of it comes from other parts of NCR. Ismail himself goes with a receipt book to the faithful in many colonies and apartments where the donors live. With such exertions are met the monthly expenses of Madrasa Jamia Naseeriya Islamia.

Incidentally, most students here have not stepped beyond Loni. The farthest anybody would have gone to is the weekly market in Ghaziabad. The market with its riot of colours, its clothes, bedsheets, shoes besides fruits seems very attractive. Most kids though are satisfied with a lemonade sold in a glass bottle. They cannot afford to buy clothes or shoes. Life is all about living within limited funds.

Back at the madrasa, they get elementary religious education. Some study to memorize the Quran, others confine themselves to a repetition after learning to read and recite the Quran. The madrasa, however, has reasons to take pride in its students. 'Eight of our kids are taking the Xth and XIIth board exams this year. Two students are pursuing their BA,' informs Ismail who, himself, has come up the hard way.

'I did my hifz and qirat from Madrasa Talim ur Rahman in Garh Mukteswar. I also completed my XII class from open school simultaneously. Then I did my BA from Maulana Azad National Urdu University through distance learning. After that I studied from Mazharul Haq Arabic and Persian University in Patna. Now I am doing MA or Fazil which is the equivalent.'

Now Ismail would like his students to follow suit. 'After doing my graduation from MANUU in 2005 I could have opted for a usual career, picked up a normal office job. However, I opted to work here to make it possible for madrasa students to pursue secular learning even as they become hafiz or do their amil or fazil course in the madrasa. It is important to have both qualifications. I am trying that the students who are interested can be helped to prepare for their board examinations, just like we do in a madrasa Sector 63 in Noida. That madrasa is relatively recent, but has made good progress.'

Madrasa Naseeriya, Loni, Ghaziabad: Republic Day celebrations

For Madrasa Jamia Naseeriya Islamia therein lies hope. In the coming years, education may not always be about bifurcation. With some effort and enterprise, the students might just find a meeting point between transmitted and rational sciences.

Jamea tul Salehat: Where Girls Are Welcomed with Pride Rampur, UP

Dr Najmus Saher
Jamea tul Salehat

Dr Najmus Saher is an Assistant Professor of Islamic Studies at Jamia Hamdard, New Delhi. In this Delhi-based university, she appears to have adapted very well, doing her job competently and at par with all other colleagues in this university or elsewhere. Meeting and interacting with her no one would believe that she started her studies from a madrasa in Uttar Pradesh.

Narrating her story, she says, 'I am a native of Basti in Uttar Pradesh. In search of a job my father moved to Rampur, another Muslim majority town in Uttar Pradesh, where I was born. At that time, most of the Muslim households were not in favour of educating girls, but my father, though a religious being, wanted to educate me. He chose to empower me with religious education and sent me to Madrasa Jamea tul Salehat in Rampur. The madrasa life was so lively and engaging that time flew past me and in 2006 I completed my graduation from my favourite madrasa. By that time, I had made up my mind to join some contemporary educational institution to catch up with changing times. I decided to move to Delhi and chose Jamia Hamdard as my next institution where I took my admission in Islamic Studies. I had studied about Islam in my madrasa but very much wanted to study in a contemporary perspective. My parents supported me because they were strong believers in educating girls. They always said that only education can really empower and enrich women'.

However, it was not all smooth sailing for the girl who had studied alongside girls only in a strictly regimented environment. For the first time, she realized she could discuss things with guys, learn alongside them. 'The initial days at Jamia Hamdard were very challenging as I was coming from a girls' only madrasa and here I was in a co-education institution with a lot of freedom. No curbs on our movement, and choice of friends, we could talk and discuss on any topic. Though I could notice a few setbacks of this environment, but its advantages were much more and in plenty. My interaction with different kinds of people, from our own as well as other universities gave me an immense exposure and awareness of our diversity. There was hardly an issue under the sun that we did not discuss and derived our own conclusions. In this motivating environment, I completed my Masters with a strong desire to continue further and join doctoral programme. But my parent's financial condition was too poor to support my further study in Delhi and bear expenses of higher education. I had, however, one hope. If I could clear the University Grants Commission fellowship exam, I will have a chance. I worked hard day and night, my family encouraged and supported me. I did not disappoint them and cleared my NET exam in the first attempt itself but missed fellowship. But it enabled me to take admission in Ph.D., which I did.'

Thus emboldened by her hard earnest success, Sehar looked to widen her vistas. The next success was not far to achieve. 'My mother used to say "God helps those who help themselves". I did see it happening when in the first year itself I got the Maulana Azad Fellowship. Now I could shelve my financial worries and focus on my studies. It was a very enriching phase of my life. I got my doctorate in 2015 on the topic "Muslim female writers on women rights: An analytical study of Maryam Jameelah, Amina Wadud and Fatima Mernissi". Incidentally, the choice of women scholars for study was itself both interesting and insightful. After all, not very many traditional families are open to the idea of accepting Amina Wadud as a scholar worth applauding. The traditionalists have scoffed at Wadud leading mixed gender Friday prayers in the USA some fifteen years ago. For her to be a subject of study for a madrasa girl shows a clear and perceptive mindset. It was a mindset open to winds of change. It enabled her to land a job too.'

'Soon after, I got the opportunity to teach as a guest lecturer at Jamia Millia Islamia, New Delhi. It gave me an opportunity to interact with faculty and students of the Department of Islamic Studies of Jamia Millia Islamia. All these exposures helped my grooming beyond my expectations. Sometimes I do reflect and find it amazing how a madrasa girl got transformed into a university teacher. What matters most is our resolve, commitment to do something and to work hard to actualize our dreams. The family support is utmost important. I could not have done anything without my family which helped me to stand up whenever I felt tumbled and tired.'

Najmus Seher is among a handful of madrasa students to have gone on to carve out a niche for themselves in regular universities

Laudable as her achievement of teaching at JMI was, Sehar refused to rest on her laurels. Soon, she added a new string to her bow; a permanent job at a place where she learnt! 'I was fortunate enough to get a permanent position of Assistant Professor at Jamia Hamdard in 2018. Now with a secure job I am focusing single-mindedly on my students and research. Whenever I go to Rampur I never forget to visit my madrasa where I am no less than a celebrity, a model for all those young girls who wish to fly high, breaking the glass ceiling. I can see the glitter in their eyes when they put their innocent questions to me. I am happy to see so many young stars ready to adorn the night sky. The dark night of women subjugation is bound to disappear—there is a morning to every night, however long it may appear and however dark it is.'

While narrating these words, she gets lost in a trail of nostalgia, at times wistful, at times, cheerful, but often lost in her emotions.

Looking back, she can afford to her a moist eye. The Rampur girl has come a long way. And finally found her true calling. For Jamea tul Salehat girls, there could scarcely have been a better role model.

. . .

Located just 70 kilometres from Rampur in western Uttar Pradesh, Kashipur is a typical small town of North India. Plenty of bustle in the market, lots of din in the morning and afternoon, before a complete calm descends post sunset. Wily-nily Kashipur found itself nudged into the Shayara Bano versus the Union of India case, popularly known as the Triple Talaq judgement. In August 2017, the Supreme Court of India invalidated instant triple talaq. Quoting from the Quran and Hadith, the learned judges felt the Talaq-e-Biddat or instant triple talaq enjoys no support from the Quran, thus stands invalidated. The judgement made national and international headlines as Bano's quest to get the final word on triple talaq ended in the landmark judgement of the Supreme Court.

Yet, it could have all been avoided had the maulanas and the muftis in Kashipur given sane advice to Bano and her father who approached them following the receipt of a talaqnama through the post. It so happened that Bano's estranged husband called her up when she was staying with her father in Kashipur following a dispute with her husband. He asked her to receive a post he had sent. A real estate agent, he claimed the document was about some property. The unsuspecting wife received it, only to get the shock of her life. The document was actually a talaqnama with the word talaq written three times. Attached was a cheque for her mehr (dower) and maintenance. Shocked, Bano and her father consulted the ulemma for a way out. The maulanas probably were not well versed with the Hanbali ruling under which multiple pronouncements of talaq at a single sitting are considered only a single, revocable divorce. Anyway, the qazis in Kashipur told Bano her marriage was over. Also, a little before the post from her husband, no local cleric told Bano how she could walk out of a violent marriage to an abusive man by opting for khula, a woman's inalienable right to divorce.

Her family consulted the local clerics, and understood there was no way out for her. Hence, she approached the Supreme Court. Well, all this could have been avoided had Bano, instead of going to the apex court in Delhi, come down just 70 kilometres or so from her residence to Rampur. Here, she could have consulted scholars of Islam who would have told her the exact position of divorce in Islam, the clerics who would have quoted from the Quran's Surah Baqarah and Surah Talaq, and not based their ruling on only a solitary instance from the life of a caliph. Bano could have even spoken to women scholars here. All this would have been possible had she even sought the counsel of the former students or staff of the half-a-century-old Jamea tul Salehat, an institution that prides itself in teaching its students to regard Islam as a way of life, and not just a series of rituals.

Unlike most madrasas which emphasize hifz alone at the initial stage, the girls' only Jamea tul Salehat introduces its students to the meaning of the Quran, the context of the divine text from the early days. Take for instance, the morning assembly at the institution. Every morning, like in most public schools, the students here stand for an assembly where one of the girls recites a Surah from the Quran with perfect intonation. This not only boosts the confidence of the students to later recite from the Quran in addressing the general public, but was also considered a revolutionary step when this practice started in the early 1970s. At that time, most girls were not encouraged to recite the Quran with qirat at home. At Jamea it was different. Once a student had recited the Surah with qirat, another stepped forward to give its translation. This little first step meant that the students here understood what they read when they recited the Quran. That is not all. The students were given easy handbooks of founder Abdul Hai and noted Jamaat e Islami scholar Yusuf Islahi. The books dealt with every-day issues of life. For instance, the provision of talaq in Islam, the share of women in property, the method of offering funeral prayers, the special prayers in Ramadan, the Taraweeh, etc. Again, former students of the madrasa recall how the institution permitted all the girl students to stand in a funeral prayer of one of their classmates who had passed away in the late

1970s. Considering, women are still, by and large, excluded from funeral prayers in India, it was again, nothing short of revolutionary to involve girl students in a funeral prayer some 50 years ago. Equally importantly, the Jamea tul Salehat charted another course uniquely its own when it encouraged its students to offer daily salat in a congregation.

Jamea tul Salehat provides a blend of Islamic and regular education to girls

Yet again, in India, women are usually advised by clerics to offer their prayers in the inner rooms of their house rather than going to a masjid for daily or Friday prayers. Same for Taraweeh, the special prayer in Ramadan. The Jamea started with daily prayers in groups for girls. Initially, there were not enough good qaris to recite the Quran with perfect intonation. So group Taraweeh was avoided. It all changed a few years ago as girls worked on their skills, and started leading an all-girls jamaat. Incidentally, the Jamea is an all-women institution. All academics are women, the examiners are women too; the men being confined to security at the gate or in the skeletal support service only. It is remarkable considering it is a big institution spread across acres of land. Unlike most madrasas for boys, this place has space for a canteen, a general store, a bank and even a small hospital. Also, the students here do not sit on the floor to learn their lessons. While most madrasas for boys still expect the students to sit cross-legged in front of their benches, Jamea has had provisions for tables and chairs for close to 50 years. Incidentally, technically it started in 1972, but the old-timers of Rampur insist it was functioning for about a decade before that with a limited number of students. Maulana Abdul Hai was the founder of the institution. Hai's aim was to come up with generations of women who will be well read, aware of their rights and responsibilities, and go on to be able mothers, sisters, daughters and wives. For him, social change had to begin with women. Feeling strongly about most madrasas not having any provisions for women, he set about establishing a special institution for women that is arguably among the best in the country today.

Jamea tul Salehat: A girl performs

Incidentally, the realization of the need for women's education was acutely felt within the community. With the cream of the Muslim society having migrated to Pakistan, those who stayed behind were educationally backward and financially enfeebled. In the early 1950s, several Jamaat-e-Islami Hind leaders who, facing periodic incarceration, realized that there were hardly any institutions which could enable the Muslim women fulfil their roles as mothers, wives or even citizens of a pluralist country. Yes, there were secular institutions where they, like anybody else, they could get admission, but there was an acute dearth of institutions which would instil Islamic values without losing sight of secular subjects like history, English, Hindi, even Sanskrit. It was during this period that Hai along with Abul Laith Islahi started a temporary madrasa for girls in a portion of a private residence in Rampur. Initially, most of the students were the children of the Jamaat leaders only. As the realization spread, people came forward a donation campaign started with a minimum donation of ₹100. Around the same time, another Muslim leader Iqbal Baji undertook a door-to-door campaign to convince people to educate their daughters. From a foot soldier of this education campaign, Iqbal Baji became the principal of the institution as more and more girls were admitted. This was around 60 years before the Government of India launched a Beti Bachao Beti Padhao campaign. In Rampur, they not only protected their daughters, they also sent them to Jamea tul Salehat for education.

For record purposes, Hai laid the foundation stone of Bachchion ka Madrasa in 1956 and set out for Hajj. In 1963, it was affiliated to AMU's high school. Seven years later, it started having a boarding system for outstation students; a sure sign of the madrasa's early success.

Today, the best compliment for it comes not from the national media which remains oblivious to this madrasa for girls, but from the well-heeled residents of Rampur. It is considered the in-thing for deendar (pious) families to send their daughters to Jamea tul Salehat for schooling; those with vision of academic excellence send them to local convent schools. Little girls from well-off families begin their education here. Dressed in smart salwar kameez and a dupatta with which they cover their head only when out in public—inside the institution, it is an all-women zone, hence no need for complete hijab. The madrasa offers the best of Islamic education but makes sure that the duniyavi (wordly) taleem (education) is not compromised. If today, the institution follows the National Council for Educational Research and Training curriculum, back in the 1970s, the preferred affiliation was to AMU, and the students here followed the syllabus followed in Aligarh schools.

Unlike the boys from madrasas who memorize the Quran without understanding a verse of it, the Jamea girls have a very different grooming. The simple, easy-to-understand books in Urdu apprise the students with more things than initially visualized. With sound grooming of religion, they are able to make their own independent decisions. Hence, no cleric is required to tell them that as women they are permitted to participate in funeral prayers—remember back in the 1970s when a girl student expired, other girls and staff took part in the funeral prayers for the departed. Or in case of divorce, there is a procedure given in the Quran; it is a procedure which nullifies instant triple talaq. It is a piece of information Bano could have done with. It is a little eye-opener that could have saved scores of women similar suffering. Jamea tul Salehat is indeed equipping women with the best weapon: knowledge. And doing so quietly, consistently, just as the Prophet had advised: a small, but consistent step is better than a big but inconsistent approach.

Jamia Aisha Niswan, Hyderabad

The city of Hyderabad is an interesting mix of old and new—not only in terms of buildings but in believers and behaviour also. The Old City is dotted with dargahs, mosques and madrasas with their accompanying ecosystems. In total contrast is new Hyderabad, the hi-tech city, a top IT hub of the country housing best of multi-national companies, malls, multiplexes, decent hangouts and what not.

Tugged away in narrow bylanes of Madannapet is Jamia Aisha Niswan, a girls' madrasa. Madannapet near old Eidgah is just like any other Muslim-dominated mohalla consisting of about 5,000 households, dotted with tea stalls, small shops and mosques but no schools or madrasas. Khwaja Nazimuddin Sabeeli, an old

For women-only madrasa Aisha Niswan in Hyderabad
aims to impart quality education to girls

resident of the area, would often discuss with his friends, the need for a girls' madrasa to provide religious education to the neighbourhood girls. One of his close friends offered his guest room for the purpose and the madrasa started with seven girls in the summer of 1986. Next year they rented a house, a part of which was converted into a make-shift hostel to accommodate out-station girls. To accommodate increasing number of girls they added rooms to the house but soon realized that they need a bigger and proper place. As there was no madrasa or school in the vicinity in this part of old Hyderabad, this upcoming madrasa was in great demand. Second, during that period, Hyderabad was facing communal turbulence. Communal strife was common and usually followed by curfew. As a norm, the interiors of city areas, particularly the mohallas were not affected by curfews and inside those narrow lanes, life remained normal. That was of much advantage to this madrasa as girls could easily move through these labyrinths to attend the madrasa. When it was decided to purchase land for the madrasa, the same locality was the first choice for this reason. To take care of future expansion, Aaisha Education Society was formed and registered. A modest-sized piece of land was bought and construction started in 1992.

Though this madrasa retains some of the features of traditional madrasas, it has introduced many innovations also. Dars-e-Nizami, the eight-year course, which is taught in most of madrasas, has been modified. The management reduced or altogether removed some of the redundant parts and introduced English and Mathematics. They admit girls who are around 11 years of age. At the time of admission, their language skills, particularly of Arabic and Urdu are tested. If they are poor or have not learnt anything prior to reporting here, they are admitted to class one, which is first year of a three-year duration Idadia, a basic course where the teacher starts from scratch. They are taught Arabic, Urdu, English, Mathematics along with some other basic religious teachings. The proper Dars-e-Nizami curricula starts from fourth year. If the new entrant has good command over Arabic and Urdu and knows elementary mathematics, can read Quran correctly, she is admitted directly to fourth year, skipping three years of Idadia. The admissions are done in the month of July, unlike other madrasas where admissions are done after Ramadan break, according to lunar calendar. Their weekly off is on Sunday, unlike Fridays in most madrasas. The madrasa starts at 8:30 am and continues till 2:15 pm without a break. Each period is of 40 minutes duration, which includes a library period also. The madrasa has a uniform of light blue shirt and white salwar. Students are introduced to computers in the seventh year of their eight-year course. After school hours, extra classes are held in the afternoon for weaker girls for almost all subjects. During the initial four years of this education they are also trained in cutting, tailoring, embroidery and cooking.

From sixth year of their education, girls are given option to appear in class tenth exam of National Institute of Open Schooling (NIOS). The madrasa has made arrangement with the Regional Centre of NIOS in Hyderabad. Those who clear their class tenth exam prepare for senior secondary exam during the last two years of their education. Most of them clear their senior secondary along with their madrasa courses. This way Jamia Aaisha Niswan ensures a dual certificate for each of its student, a feast not so common in other madrasas.

They are able to make this fusion of knowledge with a group of quite dedicated teachers most of whom are ladies. In the beginning they engaged four lady teachers, all from Malegaon area in Maharashtra. Not surprising, as the neighbourhood was largely illiterate. In subsequent years, the brilliant former students of the madrasa were engaged as teachers. Now they have a team of 40 teachers, all their own graduates.

The innovative practice of Aaisha Niswan made it quite famous and as their graduates moved to other places, the news spread far and wide. They started getting substantial number of girls, initially from neighbouring Karnataka and Maharashtra and then from as far as Kashmir, Bihar and Bengal. Now in their hostel they have students from about 12 different states of the country. Another point of attraction is their low fees structure. A resident girl pays only one thousand rupees for studies, boarding and lodging. Day scholars pay 500 bucks. When asked how they manage to make two ends meet, the principal told that all girls do not pay even this meagre amount as they come from very poor background. On an average just 30 per cent of girls pay full amount and about the same percentage pays nothing. Rest 40 per cent pay partly. The deficiency is met out by donations from neighbourhood as well as from other parts of Hyderabad city.

The principal shared it proudly that they do not send safeer (the volunteers who collect donation for madrasas or mosque) to any place. Rather people either come to them to deposit their donation or transfer to their accounts. It again reflects the goodwill the madrasa has earned.

This practical approach to impart useful and contemporary education along with basic religious teachings attracted madrasas in other states also to use their expertise and they either got affiliation or established branches in their areas.

At present, Madrasa Aaisha Niswan has 40 branches or affiliated madrasas where almost 7,500 girls are getting education. The local management uses skype and other techniques to connect with the staff and students of all these branches. Certain specialized and specific topics are taught by experts here at Hyderabad and broadcast live to all other madrasas making it a big virtual classroom.

More often than not, power point and OHP tools are used to teach students, particularly when the subject is taught by a male because males are not permitted to teach face to face. From a faraway corner in the madrasa, the male teacher communicates and shares his knowledge. When asked about this rather orthodox and strict separation, we were told that the madrasa is dealing with the kind of people who believe in strict segregation and if their sentiments are not respected they may not send their daughters for education and that would be a bigger loss. It reminded one of the good old Rabea Girls Public School in Delhi. It was started by Hakim Abdul Hameed in the Walled City. Its educational standards were at par with the best public or convent schools in the 1970s. Somebody suggested that the school could be shifted to New Delhi to provide more space for sports and cultural activities. The management declined, aware that traditional residents of Old Delhi would not send their daughters out of Old Delhi for education. A shift to New Delhi would be counterproductive, they reasoned.

Meanwhile, at Jamia Aisha Niswan, the muezzin from adjoining mosque could be heard calling for afternoon prayer. It was time to wind up and establish prayer.

Kerala Shows the Way

Kerala is the place where Islam reached during the lifetime of the Prophet. It is the state where the first mosque of India was built in 629 AD. It still continues to be more diligent and steadfast in following the precepts and practices of the Prophet. Kerala is the only state where women have an easy access to mosques. Almost all across the country, there will not be as many mosques which provide facilities to women worshippers as Kerala alone. According to an estimate, in Kerala there are more than 600 mosques of Jamaat-e-Islami Hind which provide regular access to women worshippers. Add to that a number of Salafi and Ahl-e-Hadith mosques, and you get a picture of a state which does not expect its women to say their prayers only at home. Just the way the Prophet would have had it. It is worth recalling, the Prophet asked the men not to deny women their space in mosques. Incidentally, it is not just in mosques that women can be found regularly. In the state's madrasas, schools and colleges, girls often outnumber the boys by a good margin.

In madrasas too, Kerala is way different from its counterparts elsewhere. Here, knowledge or *ilm* is not confined to a reading of Quran or the Hadith. It is all-encompassing, including as it does the latest in medicine, engineering, language, etc. The students of madrasas here do not read the Quran without understanding a word of it. They know Arabic well, often well enough to converse in the language, usually good enough to translate from say, Malayalam to Arabic or Arabic to English. They understand what the Quran says in the original. They are not always dependent on translation. It is not something that can be said about a vast majority of madrasa graduates from Bengal, Bihar, Uttar Pradesh, Rajasthan or Haryana. Nor are the madrasa graduates expected to confine their study to deen or faith; the idea being that all knowledge which is beneficial for humanity should be pursued. This approach is diametrically opposed to what many *alims* (scholars) in North India profess: madrasas' job is to provide spiritual leaders, the moral guardians for the common man; it is not their call to groom engineers or doctors, etc. Just as an engineering college or a management institute is not asked about the perceived lack of moral content in their syllabi, the madrasas should not be asked about the absence of subjects in their syllabi which would fetch them well-paying jobs, they argue. The madrasas should not be seen from the same yardstick.

Upward economic mobility is not necessarily the sole desired objective in life.

In Kerala, however, the madrasas seek to blend the two, reasoning that there is no separation of knowledge in Islam. They point out that the Prophet did not divide learning on the basis of sacred and secular. A man was expected to pursue all that is good. They remind that the Quran asks humanity to explore the world, find out the beauty of the phenomenon of human existence. It is with this mindset that the locals, particularly those owing allegiance to Kerala Nadwat ul-Mujahidin, believe there is no official clergy in Islam. Hence, there is no space for a regular imam in a masjid. A virtuous doctor or a management guru is as capable of leading prayers as a so-called professional imam. Some members actually reject the idea of a professional imam altogether. Similarly, the Friday khutba, delivered in Arabic, is translated into Malayalam, as not all worshippers are familiar with Arabic. This again is in total contrast to most states of North, East and Central India where the khutba is delivered in Arabic without translation in a local language. It is an ironical situation: in Kerala more students understand Arabic, yet the khutba is translated into Malayalam to reach the widest number of people; in North India only a few students are well versed with Quranic Arabic, and fewer still of the common populace. Yet the Friday sermon is seldom translated into Hindi or Urdu for easier and larger dissemination.

The hundreds of madrasas under Nadwat ul-Mujahidin blend religious and secular learning. There is no lack of compatibility between Islam and this worldly subjects like mathematics, logic, language and literature, etc. In their syllabus, they move away from books on Islamic jurisprudence, arguing they all were added after the time of the Prophet, and even after the end of the reign of the four caliphs. Hence, their authenticity cannot always be vouched for. They insist on returning to the Quran and the Hadith. The Mujahids also lay a lot of stress on scholarly attainments besides social work. It is not unusual to find their scholars penning works on the right of every individual to seek education, or the rights of women when it comes to education, property or matrimonial alliances. The subjects as also the tenor of these works shows a gender-neutral approach. It is a refreshing change from some of the books of North Indian scholars who, in the days gone by, used to remind women of their responsibilities, and seldom tired of talking about the rights of men! So much so that some of them approved of halala as a way of punishing an ill-tempered husband. There was no thought spared for the condition of a woman put in the ignoble situation. On the social front too, the Mujahids believe that as part of the ummah, one can to extend invitation to the larger humanity. Just as we are told through verse 125 of Surah Nahl,

> Invite all to the Way of your Lord with wisdom and holy teaching, and reason with them by ways that are the best and the most gracious: Truly your Lord knows best, (those) who have strayed from His path, and (those) who receive guidance.

Accordingly, the Mujahids engage in a lot of social work. They concentrate too on gathering zakat from well-off Muslims and use it collectively. The idea is to uplift the poor. Rather than giving a little amount to many individuals, a larger amount is given to one individual, so that he gets out of the cycle of poverty; a person who gets zakat one year should be able to, in turn, pay zakat in the coming years, thus completing the cycle of being a recipient to a donor. A small amount only helps in meeting immediate expenditure, and does not take the family out of the rut in the long run. Interestingly, some of the Nadwatul scholars believe that zakat can be given to both Muslims and non-Muslims as the Quran does not bar any needy person from availing its benefit. It is an interpretation that is widely disputed as most madrasas and *alims* across the country believe that while charity (sadqa and khairat) can be given to any needy individual, irrespective of his religion, zakat is meant only for the uplift of the faithful, so that the Muslim brotherhood is fostered, and more people can be at par.

The good work of madrasas in Kerala is not confined to Mujahids. In fact, it runs across the state and across various Muslim bodies. For instance, the work done by Jamaat-e-Islami Hind in the state. The Jamaat has consistently worked not just for gender parity, but easier dissemination of education in the state. Or by the bodies answering to the names of Samastha Kerala Jamyiathul Ulema, Dakshina Kerala Jamyiathul Ulema and Tabligi Jamaat.

The age-old Muslim body Jamaat-e-Islami Hind here far from debarring Muslim youth from entering mainstream, actively encourages them to get into journalism, medicine, engineering, etc. The JIH believes that Islam addresses the human beings as a whole; so there cannot be a segregation of learning. JIH, Kerala is the first organization in Kerala to start a women's Arabic college called Madrasathul Banath at Chennamangalloor, Kozhikode district. While this notable first is laudable, what is more admirable is that the body thought in terms of women's education.

Interestingly, the education system of these madrasas is different in Kerala. For instance, there are both morning and evening madrasas, unlike other parts of the country where an average day in a madrasa begins soon after breakfast and the first session winds up around noon. Then there are Islamiya or Arabic colleges where students seek both religious education as also secular one; the idea is to gain points both in the Hereafter and this world. At a higher level, there are Islamic universities where madrasa students are not only welcome, but are often in decision-making bodies. The only similarities to North Indian madrasas can be found in south Kerala where Deoband and Tablighi Jamaat scholars are in preponderance. Across the state there is far greater emphasis on learning English and computer education. There are plenty of institutes which offer an Islamic course under Majlissu Talimul Islami. They have a specially designed curriculum, which is a mix of subjects taught in the Islamic and general universities. Subjects such as Arabic, sociology, economics and commerce are offered at graduation and post-graduation levels. The curriculum is structured to prepare the students to get moral and modern education which will prepare them to meet the challenges of life after madrasas or colleges. The medium of instruction is either Arabic or English. There is no emphasis on Urdu, a language erroneously believed to be that of all Muslims in madrasas of Deoband in Uttar Pradesh, Rajasthan, Delhi, etc. In fact, much of the religious literature used in the madrasas in North India is in Urdu under the misguided belief that every Muslim understands Urdu. So much so that when these jamaats or Muslim organizations publish copies of the Quran in Hindi, it is usually the Urdu translation in Devanagari script! On the other hand, in Kerala there are a few institutes which follow Malayalam as the medium of instruction. Students move to English/Malayalam medium in State or CBSE schools after completing their two-hour morning madrasa. It is Kerala's counterpart to what is called maktab elsewhere. It links the regular school going children with the spiritual leanings of the community.

While there are hundreds of madrasas which are linked to colleges, and many colleges are, in turn, managed by madrasa scholars, there are some institutes which are as good as any in Muslim countries abroad. They maintain their own websites, announce new courses, vacancies, etc., like any professional institute imparting secular education. Take for instance, the well-respected Darul Huda Islamic University run by Samastha Kerala Jamiyathul Ulama as also Markazussaqafathu Sunniyya run by All India Sunni Jamiyathul Ulama. Not to forget Al-Jamia Al Islamiya Santhapuram which is run by Jamaat-e-Islami Hind with the motto of 'educating the leaders of tomorrow'. The body claims,

In 1955, the erstwhile Islamiya College Santhapuram marked a new beginning by fusing together holistic inter-disciplinary Islamic educational paradigm that combined Islamic tenets of knowledge with the futuristic secular education. This unique model set the tone and tenor for an Islamic educational renaissance in Kerala. Much has changed since then. It propelled many other institutions to shed the burdens of the past and enter a new era in Islamic education. The single biggest contribution of al Jamia was, perhaps, that it was instrumental in changing the prevailing narrative of Islamic education in Kerala. Al Jamia has, by the grace of Allah, been successful in producing a new cadre of scholars, thought leaders, da'wa workers, socio-political activists, media persons, writers and intellectuals capable of leading the community from the front.

Remarkably, when al Jamia talks of providing leaders to the community, its approach is not too different from that a traditional *alim* from Deoband or Firangi Mahal! Their destination is the same, the route quite different.

Equally upfront about its activities is Darul Huda Islamic University, a member of the Federation of the Universities of the Islamic world. Its founder was Pangil Ahmed Kutty Musliar, former president of Samastha Kerala Jamiyyathul Ulema. Important to reiterate that Jamiat, in Delhi and elsewhere, is associated with Darul Uloom, Deoband. Here, however, the approach is different, the body does not shy away from using the modern tools of communication. In Kerala, Darul Huda Islamic University happily gives its history on its site, stating,

> Tanur is the birthplace of educational inheritance of Kerala Muslims. According to documents Dars system was established in the 15th Century as Valiyakulangara mosque. Many famous scholars have taught here for many years. In that time. It was the repository Islamic education. During Malabar riot Aminummantakath Pareekutty Musliyaat, author of a revolutionary book which inspired the people to fight against the British invasions, was the teacher of this mosque. As aftermath of this riot, British police confiscated the book and exiled the author. Absence of Pareekutty Musliyar led the Dars here to the brink of ruin. According to the request of people, well known reformer Pangil Ahmed Kutty Musliyar came to Tanur and organised Asasullslam Saba and reformed Darsas Islahul Uloom madrasa in 1924. In 1931 he built a building known Baqiyaath of Malalbar thanks to its resemblance with Baqiyath Swalihath, an Arabic college in Vellore.

With such foresight and clarity, the madrasas in Kerala strive to live up to an age-old adage: There is one God; His creation is one too. So are the various forms of knowledge needed to understand this world and God. The idea here is, Islam is not a set of rituals. Rather, it is a way of life. And that way of life includes all learning as long as it contributes to advancement of humanity. The madrasas here refuse to draw false verticals of exclusion and division.

Ahl-e-Hadith Madrasas

In the shadow of the age-old Jagat cinema, the future scholars of Islam are being groomed. The road leading to Madrasa Riyazul Uloom in the Walled City of Delhi is full of eateries. There are stalls selling fried fish and chicken changezi. Others offer seekh kabab and biryani. The business is brisk. Each has its regular patrons. A few steps further down the road, you will find plenty of chickens in coops, all waiting to be sold. Unmissable in this hustle-bustle of a typical Old Delhi market are a few shops selling Urdu and Arabic books, copies of the Quran, Hadith books, rosaries, caps and prayer mats. They sell miswak (natural tooth cleaner made of tree wood) and dates too, completing the picture of a shop specializing in the stuff a practising Muslim may desire. Every now and then, one can find a calligrapher finishing a work of art at the entrance of these shops. They are an accurate barometer of what lies ahead. A few brisk steps from these traditional Islamic book shops is Madrasa Riyazul Uloom, located just a few hundred metres from the historic Jamam Masjid in Old Delhi, and within a whistling distance of Jagat cinema. The cinema which was called Nishat in the 1930s, downed its shutters nearly two decades ago. The madrasa continues to concentrate on its students, going about its business quietly, calmly and consistently. It operates out of a masjid. But what a history it carries!

Ahl-i-Hadith madrasa, Riyazul Uloom, a classroom where
students sit cross-legged on a mattress

Though it maintains a relatively low profile, this Ahl-e-Hadith
madrasa dates back to 19th century. It was built in the early 1880s,
preceding the foundation of the Congress in 1885 by a year
or two. In many ways a contemporary of both Deoband and
Nadwa in Lucknow, Riyazul Uloom has been a little stream to
their torrent. Yet, it has gone on steadily, grooming generations
of men into scholars of repute. Today, scores of its students are
practising doctors, chemists, management experts, professors and
government servants. If that seems like the resume of a university,
think again, as all these professionals are also hafiz-e-Quran (those
who have memorized the Quran), experts of Arabic knowledge
and more than conversant with the teachings and practices of
the Prophet. It is a rare combination, rarer still when one realizes
that most scholars of Deoband or its affiliated madrasas usually
confine their ilm to Islam. Here in Riyazul Uloom, there is no
segregation of the religious and the secular or the mundane.
A student is encouraged to learn what is good for this world and
the hereafter.

As its rector Aamir Abdur Rashid puts it,

We try to strike a balance. We want to attain this world as also Hereafter. Islam is not about leaving the world and confining yourself to a masjid or a madrasa. We want that a student who passes out of this madrasa should be able to look after his financial interests. It is not necessary for a madrasa graduate to be just a muezzin or an imam in a masjid. There is criticism from some ill-informed people that we neglect the teaching of the Quran and Hadith. It is not true. However, unlike the Deoband seminaries, we do not neglect material subjects. We strive to give a balanced grooming to students.

The madrasa has between 200 and 300 students at any given time, among them are Hanafis too!

In the name of 'balanced grooming' the madrasa imparts instruction in both Hindi and Urdu. It teaches English and computers as well. Interestingly, for English, it has a post-graduate of English teaching the students while maulanas take care of religious grooming. However, it does not have instructors for science and mathematics. The rector says,

The students make their own arrangements. Some opt for private tuitions. Most, however, do private study. We give them time for it. They take examinations from the National Open School. If they study with us, our certificates are recognised in Central Universities like Jamia Millia Islamia, Aligarh Muslim University, Maulana Azad National Urdu University. Jamia Hamdard also recognises our certificate. If our students want to go abroad for higher studies or picking up a job, nearly all universities in Saudi Arabia recognise our madrasa. It is the same case with many other countries in the Gulf. In Malaysia too, our madrasa is recognised. We have a limitation of space. As a result cannot do too many cultural activities. It is partly because we operate out of a masjid. But our students go places.

The students' dormitory which offers only basic facilities

Indeed, such is the reputation of the madrasa that its alims have to step beyond their usual role to sort out personal issues in the life of the faithful. The madrasa acts as an informal court where quarrelling couples bring their problems for resolution. Interestingly, here instant triple talaq has not been regarded as valid for decades. It is considered a single, revocable divorce, not the final divorce. Though it does not have any female students, it gets more khula cases than those of instant triple talaq. The alims here consider it as a mark of awakening among Muslim women that they know that Islam gives them a right to divorce through khula. Riyazul Uloom also helps in arriving at an amicable solution for any property-related dispute.

With such multi-pronged activities, the madrasa easily steps much beyond the image and actions of an average madrasa affiliated to Deoband.

Madrasa Sautul Quran Mohammadiya, Mewat

Something similar is being attempted at another Ahl-e-Hadith seminary, Madrasa Sautul Quran Mohammadiya in Pinagwa in Mewat, Haryana. Of much more recent lineage, it started as a maktab in 2005. However, within three years, it became a madrasa with residential facilities. It had then around 20 hostellers. Today, it has 270 residential students. They bring up more than 90 per cent of its students. Its rector Maulana Mushtaque informs that they have so far had 40 students becoming hafiz. At the same time, the madrasa is readying its students to take on matriculation examinations next year. It follows the National Council for Educational Research and Training syllabus for students from VI standard onwards. In lower classes, it follows the pattern of some of the private schools in small town India. If a student is hard working and gets at least 65 per cent marks in half yearly examinations, he is upgraded to the next class. So, if a child joins the madrasa at the age of eight, and has not had prior learning experience, he can expect to make up for a late start by the time he is 11 or 12.

Some of our students come after attending schools in their towns and villages. At other times, because the parents are poor or negligent towards education, they come here without prior education. Till standard Vth we make those concessions to students. For instance, if a student has learnt his Islamic lessons well, and is doing well in English, mathematics and sciences, etc., he is promoted to next class on the basis of his half yearly report card. We, however, do not do so from the VIth standard as we do not want to take a risk with our performances.

This awareness of the institute's performance, and pride in it, is quite unusual for a small-town madrasa where there is no exact time of joining. A child may be admitted in January as easily as in July. Not so here. Madrasa Sautul Quran Mohammdiya is not your everyday madrasa. Nor is Maulana Mushtaque just another Islamic teacher with a cane in his hand ready to discipline the slightest erring student. 'We have to promote a love for learning. Discipline is fine, but the student should love his studies, only then can he become an alim. The fear of the teacher does not help promote love for studies.' Indeed, many of the students are first-generation learner. They come from neighbouring villages where their houses often have no water connection, and electricity is but an occasional visitor. The houses, at times, do not even have a toilet. It is not unusual to find a curtain hung from a tree branch and a nail in the wall to give a semblance of privacy while bathing.

Under such circumstances the madrasa is trying to promote a love for learning. And as its rector happily points out, 'We have not produced any lecturers, professors, etc. It is too early. Our first batch of students will take their matriculation examination shortly. But in the limited knowledge our students have gained, many have gone to Delhi to pursue higher studies. Some have picked up jobs too. But a lot needs to be done.'

The madrasa, like a few others in the area, is aware of the growing need to pursue academics:

> After all the lynching incidents in the region, there is awareness among the madaris that we need to do more. The students who pass out of our madrasa should not have to depend on their traditional ways of earning. We do not want that our students should be just shepherds or dairy farmers. In these times when there is a risk to life for keeping cows, it is best that they are qualified to earn better paying and safer jobs with no risk to life.

Incidentally, Mewat has had a series of lynching incidents in which Muslim dairy farmers have been lynched by cow militia on mere suspicion of cow slaughter. It started with the lynching of Pehlu Khan in April 2015, and continued for next three years. Rakbar's lynching in 2018 subsequently caught international media attention with the making of a documentary.

The madrasa in Mewat is separated from the madrasa near Jama Masjid in Delhi. Yet both Ahl-e-Hadith seminaries retain the love for all encompassing learning. For them, learning is not only about memorizing the Quran by heart. It is about understanding it, then implementing it. Accordingly, there is focus on Arabic learning too. Once the Quranic lessons are imbibed, they have to be implemented in everyday life. For that reason, subjects aimed at making a better living are taught. No contradiction is felt between the precepts of faith and real life here. Of course, not all Ahl-e-Hadith madrasas in the alluvial plains of the Ganga are as diligent about pursuing all learning. Many follow the template of Deoband seminaries, and are happy to just add non-religious subjects to the syllabus without the required sincerity or provisions. However, things do get better as one cross the Vindhayas. In Hyderabad, Andhra Pradesh, Karnataka, Tamil Nadu and Kerala, the Ahl-e-Hadith sect has some of the best performing madrasas where a fine balance is struck between religious and professional learning. Some madrasas even help operate professional engineering or management institutes. Unsurprisingly, they are warmly embraced by people from other sects. As the Mewat madrasa cleric points out, 'We have around 30 students whose parents are Deobandis. However, they do not mind what we teach as long their child benefits from learning.'

Shia Madrasas

You talk of madrasas, and almost immediately, the thought of Deobandi madrasas crosses the mind. It is probably because a vast majority of madrasas in the country draw their template from Darul Uloom, Deoband. They may not have a formal affiliation to Deoband, and often Deoband may even be unaware of their existence, but they still follow the Deoband model. That is for the Sunni madrasas. Now mention the words 'Shia madrasa' and one name pops up immediately in conversation: Jamia-e-Nazmia in Lucknow. It was founded in 1890, making it the oldest Shia institution in the country, making it slightly senior to Nadwatul Uloom, the best-known Sunni seminary in Lucknow. Incidentally, Lucknow, in many ways, has been the cradle of Shia learning with many reputed Shia madrasas gracing its landscape. With Sultan-ul-Madaris and Madrasatul Waezeen keeping Nazmia company, the faithful are not short of choice.

Jamia-e-Nazmia was the brainchild of Syed Najmul Hassan. The seminary does not shy away from tracing its history, which again goes back all the way to 19th century. With a generous use of hyperbole and accolades, the seminary claims,

Behar-ul-Anwaar, an important fifth book of the Jafari sect was written by Allama Majlisi and coordinated by his pupil Allama Naymat-ullah Jazairi, a writer of 100 books. His successor, Mufti Syed Mohammad Abbas spread religious education all over India and established educational centres in different cities. His educational efforts were continued by his, pupil, son-in-law, and successor Syed Najmul Hasan. (His) services are spread all over the 20th century. Some prominent ones include: Changing Majlise Sadrus Sudoor into

All India Shia Conference with the help of great Shia Ulemas of the time, foundation of Shia College, Lucknow, Imam-ul-Madaris Inter college in Amroha, UP and Madrasatul Waizeen with the cooperation of Maharaja Mehmoodabad. Played an important silent role in the freedom struggle of India. In continuation, nearly 118 years ago, a madrasa in the name of Mashare-ush-Sharai was established. Later on due to cooperation of late Abbas Ali Khan it was named after his father as Madrasa-e-Nazmia.

Today, Nazmia provides free of cost education. The students are provided complimentary food and lodging. They are given scholarships too. This is a nice little concession to contemporary times. While the basic education, including knowledge of Hindi and English, is of nine years and is related to Madrasa Nazmia, the higher education is of 10 years, it comes under Jamia-e-Nazmia and includes Persian and Arabic education imparted, as per the Arabic and Persian Board of UP government. In the lower classes, mark sheets and certificates are issued. Diploma and Degrees are awarded under Munshi, Maulvi, Kamil, Alim, Qabil, Fazil and Mumtazul-Afazil. Syllabus is claimed to be the combination of the experiences of past and present learned ulamas with modern touches, which includes Aqaid, Diniyaat, Qurn, Urdu, Hindi, English, Mathematics, Geography, Science, Arabic, Persian, Mantiq, Philosophy, Hait, Urooz, Kalam, Ma-ani-wa-Bayan, History, Tafseer, Hadees wa Usool-e-Hadees and Fiqh wa Usool-e-Fiqh. Computer education is also imparted.

Then there are notable Shia seminaries like Sultan-ul-Madaris, Madrasatul Waezeen, both in Lucknow, besides Jawwadia Arabic College in Varanasi, Madrasa-e Eimania Nasiriya, Jaunpur, Najafiah, Najafi House, Mumbai and Jamia-tush Shaheed, Delhi, which all offer education that goes beyond mere religious rote learning. Aimed at grooming well rounded individuals, they offer mathematics, English, science and computer education to their students. Thereby comes a distinct departure from the practice of many Sunni institutes.

Keeping a niche all its own is Jamia Imamia Anwarul Uloom in Allahabad, which is the brainchild of Allama Zeeshan Haider Jawadi. Its stated mission is to 'To spread the light of the teachings of Quran and Prophet and his Ahl-al-bait.' The 30-year-old madrasa operates on Dars-e-Nizami method. It does not confine itself to rote learning of the Quran. It seeks to spread its overall message. In many ways, it is a new age madrasa. It claims, 'A madrasa is there to impart knowledge and educate the society; and education teaches love and mercy.'

However, in some of the smaller madrasas of the Shia community, there is only token secular education, as they like, unorganized Sunni madrasas, limit themselves to teaching the Quran and Hadith to students. Of course, there is special emphasis on the life of the grandsons of the Prophet, Hassan and Hussain. The story of Karbala is oft-repeated, thus preparing the students for the Moharram majlis later on. Otherwise, the small madrasas for Shias are often like their Sunni counterparts: a neat rectangular structure with a dome at the centre, a courtyard with rooms on one side. The hostels, however, offer more than basic amenities. It is not unusual to find beds for students, even shelves for storing their books, clothes and other belongings. There are hardly any Shia madrasas which expect the students to sleep on the floor, or to stay happy with a monotonous lunch of dal-chawal (lentils-rice) or a plain cup of tea in the morning with a toast. The fare they offer is varied, and more nutritious.

However, that is merely at the individual level. At the larger level of the community, the Shia madrasas in India lag behind badly in comparison to some of the best madrasas in Iran. There, complete knowledge of mathematics and science is imparted alongside religious instruction. And the madrasa clerics are politically aware, active and alert. In India though madrasas tend to operate in a political vacuum. As a noted journalist recalled about Tablighi Jamaat at the time of Emergency. The then Prime Minister Indira Gandhi asked about the rise of the Jamaat. Her advisors told her not to worry. 'They worry only about what is beyond the skies, or below the earth. They have nothing to do with this world.'

While this may not be strictly true about Shia madrasas, there is, however, an abiding feeling that the madrasas tend to work in an anonymous fashion, leaving the stage free for some self-appointed Shia leaders to run riot. Remember the words of Rizvi with respect to madrasas and terrorism?

I have been sent only as a teacher

—PROPHET MUHAMMAD (PBUH)

Chapter 5

INSIDE A MADRASA: A PAINTING OF A TEACHER AND HIS PUPILS

Mohammad Ali
Madrasa Darul Uloom Hashmatiya, Pilibhit, UP

It is not easy being a madrasa student in a secular society. Across vast stretch of north India, madrasa students often attract curious glances. It is as if they do not quite belong to a society used to seeing boys dressed in smarts trousers and shirt on their way to school. The madrasa students with their crumpled kurta–pyjama, plastic chappals and a worn-out bag hung around the shoulder present a different picture altogether. Then there are those who look at them with suspicion. Once, Mohammed Ali was at Lucknow Railway Station on his way to his madrasa in Pilibhit when he noticed some cops giving him a close look. The policemen asked him to open his bag, checked his belongings, and once satisfied, let him go. It was an experience that shook Ali completely.

'I remember the incident. It was in 2007. I was going to join Madrasa Darul Uloom Hashmatia in Pilibhit. I was very young at that time. My beard had not grown at that time. I saw two-three police-men with dogs, they were patrolling the platform. They came to me and asked me to open my bag. It was a shocking thing for me. I was a young student. I was alone there. I opened my bag which had only my kurta-pyjamas. They saw and went away. I come from Bundelkhand which is a Hindu majority area. People would see my outfit there and give me curious looks. I felt as if I did not belong there. My madrasa in Bundelkhand was called Darul Uloom Mohammadiya. I felt the odd one out.'

The challenge was not limited to the larger society. Inside the madrasa things were not much better. Recalls Ali,

'I have studied in eight madrasas. In all madrasas we had to sleep on floor. I have been only to smaller madrasas, not to the bigger ones like Deoband or Mubarakpur. Everywhere, the students are expected to sleep on the floor. Even in big madrasas beds are not provided. You are expected to bring your own sheets, your own utensils. They do not provide anything. The food is of not good quality. In Kanpur madrasa, the food was better. In Lucknow's Madrasatul Madeena where I studied in 2008–2009, the madrasa did not have a kitchen facility. We had to collect food from different houses in the neighbourhood. It is an old practice. The houses in the mohalla provide food by turn to the madrasa. We had to go to collect the food.'

Mohammed Ali studied at various madrasas of Uttar Pradesh before discovering his true calling at Jamia Millia Islamia

As for the syllabus, for long, people have talked of the need for a change in the syllabus. But it does not seem to register with the madrasa authorities. For instance, they still teach Persian as a religious language of Muslims whereas it was merely the court language of the Mughals.

'When the British came, they found there were two elite languages, Arabic and Persian. When Dars-e-Nizami was established—the madrasas adhere to the way established by Nizamuddin—it followed the two dominant languages. When Darul Uloom was founded, it had no choice. They did not think of Persian as a foreign language. They retained Persian books as barkat as the authors were widely respected.'

But did it not strike them that the language had extremely limited use in the outside world? The days of Persian being a court language were long since over. The job prospects did not improve significantly due to the knowledge of Persian.

'That you can say about the madrasa system as such! It does not prepare you for getting a job, etc.'

Understandably, Ali decided to leave madrasa system after getting the degree of alim, and came to Jamia Millia Islamia for his graduation. Again, it was not without hiccups. Some of the madrasa students are often told by their teachers to shun the outside world, and retain their perceived purity.

'When I told my teacher in madrasa that I was joining Jamia, he said, no it was not a good idea. The ulemma think the universities corrupt young minds. But it was not a new thing. Before me, others had been told the same too. And remember there were madrasa graduates who joined Aligarh Muslim University, and started questioning Islam. This notion emerged from there'

Indeed. Well-known Islamic scholar Yoginder Sikand had alluded to the same thing in his work *Bastions of the Believers*. Quoting a graduate of the well-respected Jamiatu-ul Falah in Azamgarh, he wrote,

Some ulama argue that if the madrasa students go to universities they would lose their Islamic character. They would begin to drink alcohol and smoke, and wear Western clothes. They would stop saying their prayers and keeping their fast in Ramadan. I don't agree with this argument at all. If madrasa students are given proper intellectual and spiritual training and their faith is firm and secure, there is no reason why this should happen. In fact, I know of many madrasa students who are now studying and teaching in universities in India and abroad. They are still as good Muslims as they were when studying in the madrasas.

Did Ali miss madrasa after joining Jamia?

'Pray, no! For the first few days, I used to get nightmares about madrasas. But today, in retrospect, I am more calm, and realize there is much that I have gained from the madrasas.'

Indeed. Today, Ali is pursuing his PhD from Jamia. The days of being looked at with suspicion by policemen and fellow civilians are long since gone. Today, he dresses up like anybody else—jeans, T-shirt, trousers-shirt. His beard is the only giveaway of his religion. Other than that with his power of expression, ease with English language, and a clear head, he could be just another educated young man in Delhi. For good measure, after madrasas, he has not only worked on his language skills—he knows Hindi, Urdu, English, Arabic and Persian—but also on his technology skills. He maintains a blog too, and is happy to revisit his madrasa days. 'There should be something I should be able to do for madrasas. I feel sympathetic towards them now. There are some madrasas which are doing good.'

. . .

The world of the traditional Indian madrasa is a unique island by itself. At a time when education is often reduced to commerce, here is a system that has kept alive the age-old *guru–shishya* parampara. Most students do not pay a fee; most teachers are paid a pittance. Right from the day a boy joins a madrasa—often with unlettered parents at home—the ustad gets down to shaping him to be an alim, groom him to be part of the larger ulemma. The aim is to provide moral leadership to the community in particular and the society in general. To see an ustad working on a shagird (pupil), getting him to pronounce his 'fa' and 'qa' correctly is to see a sculptor at work. Bit by bit rough edges are smoothened out. Then the youngster is taught about a perceived golden age of Islam, the time of the caliphs. Also told in some detail is the Prophet's administration when he conquered Medina, how the Jews, Christians and polytheists were all incorporated into the administration and how they were part of the army too. The idea behind sharing all this is to tell the new admission that the Prophet was not opposed to a multi-religious society and he used no force in spreading Islam. Anybody was guaranteed not just the right to life and to practice his religion but also a chance to serve the state as long as he was a law-abiding citizen. Of course, the little passage about the golden age is thrown in to arouse similar dreams and aspirations in the young man; that that age has to be revived, and he has to strive towards it. Some may call it indoctrination; others regard it as merely passing on the knowledge from one generation to another. So by the time a youngster is hafiz or alim from a madrasa, he is said to be ready to assume the role of moral leadership of the world.

The years he spends in a madrasa are often shaped by the personal rapport between the teacher and the taught. It is a small circle of students and teachers, both often live on the same campus 24×7. The teacher usually knows what is happening in the student's life, his family, its finances. Often the student would have an elder brother helping out the father at the family shop. Or a younger sibling going to a local private school, happily called something like Evergreen Public School or St Mother Teresa Public School! In parts of North and Central India, it is quite common for a family to send one child to the madrasa for Islamic education while the others go to the so-called secular schools with dreams of becoming doctors or engineers. For the family, it is like reserving one child to work in the path of Allah. The poorer families, of course, do not have much choice. Madrasas offer free boarding, lodging, education. Not just midday meals about which a lot is heard on the media, but three daily meals for students without charging a penny. Without any formal parent–teacher association or regular meetings with the parents about a child's progress, the parents know the child is in good hands. It is a relationship of mutual trust where the parents usually do not object to physical punishment for their child, trusting the decision of the ustad. It is a trust well earned. The ustad is not just a teacher but also a confidant, a counsellor. Often he is the only window available to a student to know about his own career prospects. In some cases, the ustad even acts as an emergency money bank for the student. Like when a student has to go home for Ramadan break and he does not have the money to book a ticket, the ustad usually puts in a word with some of the devotees who come there, and the student is helped out with his ticket. It is the same in winter if the student cannot afford a nice warm quilt on his own.

The ustad ends up playing a moral guardian too. Every night, in the absence of a warden, he takes a round of the students' premises to see if everybody has gone to sleep, or are some students stealthily watching a music video or a Shah Rukh Khan film on their mobile. In such cases, a rebuke follows. A repeat means the gadget is confiscated. Interestingly, the ustad takes a lenient view if the students are caught catching up with cricket scores, or engaging in an animated debate about the relative merits of Mahendra Singh Dhoni and Virat Kohli. Between cinema and cricket, the latter is the lesser evil in the world of traditional madrasas.

In this relationship between the teacher and the taught where the teacher goes much beyond his brief of completing the syllabus on time—usually in the month of Shabaan, a little before Ramadan—the student too does his bit which is beyond the regular duty. For instance, the students almost regularly do the washing and cleaning for the ustad. The teacher may himself be staying in a one-room accommodation without his family. So the students run errands for him, help in keeping his premises clean, take care of his laundry, etc. They even press his feet or massage his scalp as when called to do so. This despite the fact that the same teacher earlier in the day may have administered a few tight slaps to the erring student for not revising his lesson, or even made him squat like a rooster—a particularly painful and humiliating position, increasingly out of favour in school. The students too are expected to dress up in a loose kurta–pyjama, and keep a beard once the first sign of puberty hits them. Any western attire is frowned upon. Also, small aberrations like drinking water while standing, or running across the premises are often met with physical punishment—students are taught to walk like the Prophet, drink water the way he taught the faithful to do, eat the way he taught, etc.

Yet it is also a system which encourages 0 per cent dissent or deviance from the script. Forget debate or dissent, even dialogue is not particularly encouraged. The teacher's word is final, no questions asked. Remarkably, it is a system that runs on faith. The teachers are provided zero training in teaching or counselling. Usually they are themselves fresh pass out of the same madrasa, having done an alim or fazil course after their hifz. The recruitment is through word of mouth as vacancies are seldom advertised—most non-affiliated madrasas have neither the resources to insert advertisements in local newspapers nor do they pay enough to make the job appear attractive. In fact, poor salary is one constant in most madrasas with the salary of a teacher ranging from ₹5,000 to ₹8,000 depending on the location of the madrasa; a madrasa in a metropolis will usually pay higher than the one in a small town or village. Even then, this salary is not sufficient for the teacher to survive with dignity. The income is then augmented either from farm earning back home. Or, as increasingly happens in urban areas, every evening the teacher goes door to door in middle-class colonies to teach the Quran to children of well-off parents. The parents in almost all the cases would have enrolled the child in an expensive public school but would like the child to learn how to read the Quran in the Arabic original. Hence, the services of a local imam or madrasa teachers are availed. Even there, the madrasa teacher is not paid much beyond ₹1,000 per month for enabling the child to know how to read the Quran for about half an hour every day of the month with a weekly off thrown in. No hikes, no holidays, just the same routine all through the year.

This kind of job comes with a short perishable date; as a child finishes one or two readings of the Quran, the teacher is dispensed with after a token gift. He has to resume his search for another family with a child!

As for the talib-e-ilm or shagird, things are not much better. After doing his fazil course, he can at best hope to join the same madrasa as a teacher—this, in fact, is a dream job for many; teaching in the madrasa where they were taught. Many others go on to be imams or even muezzins in some masjids. Nowadays, some try to go to the Gulf where the money is infinitely better for an imam or even somebody pursing lower level usual jobs of a teacher in a school or even an accountant or a secretary. A handful try for higher education, all the time running on two parallel tracks of Islamic education and secular education. Thus, they do their BA, MA, etc. from distance education even as they pursue higher learning in a madrasa, or after moving out of the madrasa. It entails more years without any earning.

Once they are ready with these degrees to back up their madrasa accomplishments, they often realize, the world has moved on. Their limited or no knowledge of computers, accountancy, commerce or economics means they cannot compete for the best-paying jobs. Also in the absence of knowledge about different sects of Islam—most madrasas confine themselves to teaching the wards only about the sects they follow; a well-off man from a particular sect donates land, appoints teachers of the same sect to teach Islam from the perspective of their sect to children of the same sect—and zero idea about parallel religion, they are not quite equipped for moral leadership they believed they were being groomed for. The lessons of life are much harder than those of intonation and pronunciation inside the madrasa. The madrasa is, at best, an echo chamber. The voice of the world outside is quite different.

As noted Islamic scholar Prof Ishtiaque Danish, quoting a madrasa student, said at a national seminar on 'Madrasa and Educational Needs of Indian Muslims',

When we madrasa graduates enter the practical, mundane world we feel that our share in the new global village can only be on the margin. Here, the rules of the game are different and we have not learned about them at our religious seminaries. In the job market our qualifications do not carry any weight. We are completely at a loss. Where can we go and what can we do? Probably, we cannot do much except begging. But that too is no easy task especially for those who carry big dreams of changing the world.

The seeking of knowledge is obligatory upon every Muslim.

—PROPHET MUHAMMAD (PBUH)

NURTURING LIVES

Anwar Ali Khan
Madrasa Rasheedia, New Delhi

Anwar Ali Khan, a man in his early 40s, stopped his auto rickshaw at Madrasa Rasheedia on Bahadur Shah Zafar Marg in New Delhi. The madrasa, housed within the medieval mosque, Masjid Bhoori Bhatyari, was not quite the place to expect many customers. Most of those who came here for prayer worked in the vicinity. The students of the madrasa were almost all hostellers. Yet Khan waited in his auto rickshaw for a few minutes before a boy approaching teenage rushed to him. Khan gave him ₹50. The youngster was thrilled. Later, a little chat with the boy called Sohail revealed he was Khan's son. Khan comes here every day to catch up with his son for a few minutes. There are times his mother sends him some snacks and pickles. There are times his father picks up a kurta to hand over to him. On other days, he just gives him his mobile phone for a few minutes. Sohail calls up his mother, speaks to her. Then has some moments of easy banter with his younger brother Hashim and elder sister Ruqaiya. A little conversation followed immediately by a quick glance at WhatsApp messages is all he is allowed. Yet, in these few minutes he finds joy. Otherwise, Sohail misses his family. His mother, brother and sister are there in Behror in Rajasthan. Only Sohail stays at the madrasa in Delhi. His father stays with his elder brother, Sohail's uncle, a few kilometres away in east Delhi's Jagatpuri. The two brothers go back to Behror over the weekend. That is the time Sohail feels the loneliest, knowing in the big bad city of Delhi, there is nobody to call his own. Yet, Sohail is not the only one. In rural belt of the country, it is pretty common for a family blessed with many children, to send one of the sons to a madrasa. The idea is, he would go on to be a scholar of Islam, and earn marks on the scale of piety not just for himself, but his family, particularly, his parents. While other sons pursue this worldly vocations like engineering, commerce and management, etc., one child is hand-picked to be sent to a madrasa. He is seldom the first-born. The first child is invariably held back by parents. He is their post-dated cheque. The sooner he settles down after his studies the better it is for the parents. The madrasa pass-out are not exactly renowned to be money spinners. Also, girls are seldom sent away to a madrasa, the reason being as much about the absence of easy availability of a girls' seminary in a small town, as the security factor in another city. So, it is usually the youngest son, or the one in the middle in the sibling order, who is sent to a madrasa. It is, in some unique way, similar to what many practising Hindus do in northern India when the food is prepared at home. While the mother makes chapattis for everybody, she reserves one roti for the cow. The idea, again, is to earn a few points on the scale of piety. Here, a son is reserved for purposes of faith. Just like how Anwar Ali Khan and many, many others do. One son for faith, others for the world.

. . .

At the same time, boys like Sohail are among the more privileged lot. In a madrasa in contemporary India, outside of Kerala, most students hail from a poor or extremely poor background. Many are born to parents who cannot afford to give them two meals a day, forget education. Others have parents who are both poor and unlettered. So a madrasa which gives the incentive of free boarding and lodging besides education seems undeniably attractive. In fact, many students come to a madrasa for free education, free food and accommodation. They may not necessarily be looking to be scholars of Islam in the first place. It is with this segment of first-generation leaders that the madrasas play their most laudable role.

In medieval India, the best of nobles and aristocrats sent their children to madrasas to study the Quran and Hadith besides logic, mathematics, philosophy, poetry, literature, etc. They imbibed the essence of Arabic and Persian grammar which helped them gain employment with the royalty. The poor people or the local converts to Islam were few and far between. Otherwise, madrasas were a monopoly of the ashrafs, the well read and groomed, supposed upper castes in a faith that respects no caste system.

If any non-Muslims came to madrasas, they were from the upper caste Hindus, usually Brahmins. It was all upper caste, upper class structure. In modern India today, the profile of madrasas has undergone a complete transformation. Not only do the madrasas concentrate their energies more on teaching religion, but also perfunctorily make space for other subjects, their syllabus too has not been revved up for years. The teachers are poorly paid as well. Still the biggest change is that the students come from the poor segment of the society. No longer do the well read and the well placed send their kids to madrasas. Many of the talib-e-ilm of madrasas are first-generation learners. The madrasas with their very obvious limitations groom them to be responsible citizens. The madrasa degrees and certificates may not get them jobs in the market, but they do get them respect in the larger society. Further, they become a kind of aspiration figure for their larger family. As their parents would not have gone to a school, a child from such a family going on to be an alim or a hafiz means the entire family can hope for upward social mobility. The boy, in turn, becomes a role model for the youngsters in his extended family and neighbourhood. And in cases where there are multiple siblings, with some of them pursuing secular learning at either government schools or private ones, an alim in the family still helps to give a well-rounded perspective to the family. The idea is the family does not concentrate on this world bounties alone. It cares too for the afterlife. Hence, a son is admitted to a madrasa from where he passes out with a fazil degree. When this son goes back from the madrasa to his small-town home, he often starts another madrasa, thereby helping in percolation of literacy. Of course, his success story, however short, gives local Muslims a sense of identity. It is particularly relevant in stretches of Haryana and Rajasthan where Muslims and Hindus have similar names, lifestyle, etc. Only their modes of worship are different. So a family with an imam gets greater social acceptance and regard.

The madrasas at another level play a role similar to anganwadis. The students are provided not only free education, including books prescribed for their syllabus, but also free meals. A family which is hardly able to provide simply dal roti to its members is happy to know that a son gets to have a non-vegetarian meal once in a while. Also, as the working hours of a madrasa are long, and vacations are limited, it helps in instilling a sense of discipline in the young ones. For students who would otherwise be wasting their time standing at town squares, madrasas enable them to utilize it more usefully. The boys who could have fallen foul to temptations, such as drinking, gambling, etc., are given a religious grooming which goes a long way in preventing crime. Interestingly, madrasas also help in controlling ambition as the students are frequently told that this life is like an examination hall. Pass this exam in this life and move on for real life that awaits you. This may negate ambition, but it also keeps at bay moral nihilism.

For first-generation students, madrasas provide another spin-off. Once the elder sibling finds his feet here, the younger ones too end up seeking admission. And the family is quite happy to send them to a place where they would learn how to recite the Quran, and also maybe in the years to come, go on to be an imam in some mosque of rural India—the students are constantly trained in madrasas to give azaan, the prayer call, and at times even lead the prayer when the teacher is absent. It is a long process, one that takes up to eight or even nine years. Yet it is in these years that a student's mind is completely moulded, and he is told about the benefits of life lived with self-restraint. It is the same teaching that a madrasa product seeks to imbibe in his students when he grows up. It carries on from generation to generation. Sadly what also goes on from generation to generation is the complete disconnect between the madrasas and the job market. While most madrasas claim they do not prepare their students for the job market—many, in fact, want them to be messengers of Islam, leaving the livelihood matters to Almighty—the fact is, in the absence of assimilation in the job market, the students feel adrift. Many are known to pursue secular learning alongside their Islamic education. It helps to mitigate the sense of loss. While some become imams or muezzin, others join the same madrasa as a faculty member. Still others eke out a living by giving private tuitions of the Quran to children in middle-class families.

Madrasas in 21st century India may be hundreds of years removed from their heydays when scientists and imams were not mutually exclusive terms. But even in the autumn of their life, they continue to shine light on the faithful, preparing many to be the moral leaders of tomorrow, and all to be responsible, law-abiding citizens of India, one who will stand up for their rights, who will not brook exclusion based on religion, but who will also hoist the Tricolour in Independence and Republic days. Their help gives a sense of identity to their students. They give not just an Islamic identity to their pupils, but also help enrich Indian culture, thereby providing a good synthesis of Indo-Islamic culture. As noted Islamic scholar Manzoor Ahmad has written in *Islamic Education: Redefinition of Aims and Methodology*,

> The Deeni madaris in India in the last 200 years have played a role which has no parallel in history. When the British imperialists occupied this country, they drove away the Muslims not only from the seats of political power but also from other areas of influence. In those turbulent times, the problem of maintaining and deepening the Islamic identity of the recently converted Muslim masses was a formidable task. And this task fell upon ill-organised and poor ulemma in the country.

As Mohammad Iqbal said,

> Let these maktabs be as they are. Let the poor Muslims' children study in these madrasas. Had there not been these mullahs then what would have been, do you know? Whatever will happen I had all seen by my own eyes. If the Indian Muslims are deprived of the influence of those madrasas, they will face a situation like that of Muslims in Spain where in spite of 800 year Muslim rule one does not find even a trace of Muslims except the monuments of Cordoba, Grenada and Al-Hamra.

True and laudable as the role of the madrasas is in giving elementary knowledge of the Quran and Hadith to first-generation leaders, imagine the consequences if they had concentrated equally on the latest in the world of science and mathematics, like in the centuries of yore?

The ink of the scholar is more holy
than the blood of a martyr

—PROPHET MUHAMMAD (PBUH)

Chapter 7

STEPPING BEYOND THEIR USUAL ROLE

Mohsin Raza Khan
Jamiatul Falah, Azamgarh, UP

Khudi Ko Kar Buland Itna Ke Har Taqdeer Se Pehle
Khuda Bande Se Khud Puche, Bata Teri Raza Kya Hai

When Mohsin Raza Khan dared to dream, not many of his class-mates pursuing Alimiyat at Jamiatul Falah in Azamgarh gave him a ghost of a chance. He had spent seven years at the madrasa (1994–2001) and not come across one senior he could turn to for inspiration in the field of journalism. Yet journalism, and English journalism at that, is what he intended to pursue. As he set about pursuing his ambition, he did a stock taking of his assets and drawbacks. While his ability to last the distance was unquestioned, probably stemming from years of rigorous discipline the madrasa instilled, his command over English was not exactly desirable. So, after madrasa, he enrolled for BA in Communicative English at AMU, topping it up by doing Master's in English Language Teaching from the same university. If Khan had limited his dreams to his post-graduation, his would still have been a remarkable journey. He was not done though. In the heart of hearts, he wanted to see his name, his byline appear in a national daily. An opportunity came his way in late October 2008. He took an entrance test at *The Hindu*, and managed to clear it! The result surprised him as much as journalism students from AMU who had taken the same test. Though not many said it in as many words, there was an unex-pressed air of condescension about them. Not many believed that a madrasa student with no English or public-school background or even a journalism degree could clear the test at *The Hindu*. Well, Khan proved them wrong. 'The papers of English for Print Media and English for Electronic Media that I studied in BA helped me in joining *The Hindu*,' he analyses a decade later.

He, however, was not destined to be a journalist for long. In came a lucrative offer from King Khalid University in Saudi Arabia, and Khan started working as a lecturer in Department of English, Faculty of Languages and Translation in the university. Today, he waxes eloquent about his accomplishments,

'I have been working on many committees and positions in Faculty of Languages and Translation. For example, Supervisor of E-Learning Unit, and a member of Academic Development and Quality. I am certified by Quality Matters (QM) Program, USA, as QM Online Facilitator, QM Master Reviewer and QM Peer Reviewer. I have reviewed many online academic courses. I have also designed English online courses. I have completed the Certificate in English Language Teaching to Adults (CELTA) from London, UK. The CELTA is awarded by the University of Cambridge's assessment organization, Cambridge English Language Assessment (formerly known as Cambridge ESOL).'

Mohsin Raza has come a long way from the days of attending a madrasa in eastern Uttar Pradesh to teaching in Riyadh

Looking back, Khan feels, his early days at the madrasa, far from restricting his world or worldview, provided him the academic rigour and discipline for higher pursuits.

'I belong to a middle-class family. My father runs a small business of furniture in Pilibhit. We are two brothers and one sister. My parents sent my elder brother to a convent school and sent me to a madrasa because they wanted one of their children to get English education and the other Islamic education. They chose me for Madrasa, Jamiatul Falah. My madrasa days were very hectic. I had to get up early in the morning for Fajr prayer. I had to recite the Quran and get ready for my classes. I used to finish classes by Zuhr prayers in the afternoon, around 1 pm. After Zuhr, I used to have "qailula" (siesta) for half an hour. Then I used to complete my homework by Asar prayers (around 5 pm in summers). The time between Asar and Magrib (sunset) prayers was allocated for playing and outing. After offering Asar prayer, I used to play football or volleyball. Sometimes, I used to go outside the campus if I needed anything. After Isha (the last prayer for the day), it was time for dinner. After that, I used to study for the next day's lesson. It was a common practice in my madrasa that students were asked to prepare for the following lesson before starting the actual lesson. I used to sleep around 11 pm. This watertight schedule taught me discipline and punctuality. Having said this, I must confess, the facilities were somehow satisfactory at the madrasa. There were three hostels. Each hostel had big rooms. In the junior section and some classes of senior section we used to sit on woven mats on the floor. But at the higher level, there were chairs and tables in the classroom. Jamiatul Falah has taken care of both my personality development and excellence in religious education with a little amalgamation of modern subjects like English and Economics. During my madrasa days I was interested in reading Urdu and English newspapers. I used to write in weekly wall magazines of the madrasa. I had the perception that the media presents a wrong image of Muslims and Islam. I thought there were few Muslims in journalism, especially English journalism. I made up my mind to pursue courses that could help me in joining English journalism. I also thought that English journalism could give me better life in terms of earning and at the same time I could serve my community. After completing Aalimiyat from Jamiatul Falah I heard about Aligarh Muslim University (AMU) from my seniors. I did not join any coaching institute for getting admission in AMU. I personally visited AMU and its different departments. The AMU environment and its hostel culture impressed me and I decided to take admission here. In my madrasa, I was fortunate to attend lectures of guest speakers. The speakers used to point out the educational conditions of Indian Muslims and their backwardness. From that time I had decided that in future I would not be just a simple Maulvi. I would do something that I could be proud of myself, my family and my community. I would study such courses that could give me bright future and help my community to uplift. As a madrasa student, I did not have much choice of subjects except art and science streams. Since my madrasa days I was interested in English language. When I looked at the syllabus of Communicative English, its contents impressed me. I decided to take admission.

"During the first year of the graduation, the news presentation style and the language of *The Hindu* newspaper fascinated me. I used to read the newspaper from page 1 to page 16 every day for improving my English. I did not sleep until I finished the whole newspaper. From then it was my dream to join *The Hindu* newspaper." Then life gave Khan a bonus with an opportunity to work at King Khalid University. Today, the Azamgarh madrasa seems just the springboard he needed in life to make a splash!'

. . .

In many of our cities and bigger towns, the good old madrasas play a role they were never supposed to, or trained for. While most well-off Muslims do not send their children to study here, except in Kerala, most maintain a certain connect with madrasas. While some people confine themselves to donating a few rupees to a madrasa representative often seen sitting at the threshold of a mosque, most fix up a monthly endowment for a madrasa in the vicinity, or at times, far off too. Donating to a madrasa as part of sadqa, khairat or zakaat is part of charity for a pious Muslim.

It all starts off the same way. A common Muslim goes to a mosque for Friday prayers or on a Sunday to a local mosque. At the conclusion of a prayer, a man rises to make an announcement. He is a representative of a madrasa. Briefly in a sentence or two, he talks of the problems confronting the madrasa. Almost invariably, the problems are the same: shortage of food for students, absence of blankets in winter or paucity of funds for a madrasa that might finally be moving from an asbestos-sheet roof to a proper ceiling. The reaction of the assembled men is predictable too; while most leave the premises quietly at the end of the prayer, some men stay on to hand over a little amount to the madrasa representative. The chances are, if the man gives more than, say ₹100 or so, the representative would ask for his address or phone number. Then he would use it to establish link with the donor, and fix up a monthly amount for his madrasa. Often this amount is a token one. But considering the representative—usually a madrasa teacher, occasionally, a senior student—goes to around 40 such apartments or houses, he ends up making a few thousand at the end of the month. This fund is then used to finance the madrasa expenditures, from providing food and maybe blankets to students to clean drinking water, and even the salaries of the teachers.

In Ramadan when every good act is believed to get 70 times the reward of an ordinary day, the madrasa representatives get really busy, going from one colony to another, one mosque to another. Many even end up sleeping over for a night at a local mosque. The idea is to contact as many people as possible for a donation. The donors too are at their generous best in Ramadan. The donor believes he has deposited an amount for the Hereafter, the madrasa representative is happy that the expenses of this life can be taken care of for sometime. This kind of community funding is a well-organized method to make sure that every madrasa is able to provide for at least the basic needs of its students, and also pay the teachers on time. Some rich or pious people step beyond lending a token amount. They step forward to get an entire ceiling made, or even the addition of a room or two. Others help out with fans or air coolers. In smaller places, and even in the traditional walled cities, the locals contribute a fixed amount of rice, dal or wheat for the madrasa students every month. Interestingly, the food for the teachers, and occasionally for their students too, is in some places provided by residents in the neighbourhood. The residents take turns to send lunch and dinner to the madrasa teacher or a masjid imam. While most send over the food tray themselves, in some cases, the madrasa students go over to collect the food for themselves and also their teachers.

With such informal and basic ways of donations, the madrasa funds should always be above board. It does not quite happen that way. There are instances when a madrasa is floated with the idea of collecting funds, not providing education. In such cases, the so-called madrasa proprietors look for healthier donations from abroad. They add a small sum locally collected. Then a tiny madrasa is launched for namesake, or the man just disappears. As most of the donors give money in good faith, not many try to find out the use to which their funds are put. However, as some of the more careful donors discover, not everybody and everything is transparent, or trustworthy. Many of the people asking for money for a madrasa do so for one that is not there at all! Or the number of students may have been jacked up manifold to collect more funds. In fact, the authors called up at least 10 madrasas of Delhi and Uttar Pradesh from the phone numbers given on their donor receipt books. But representatives at only two madrasas answered the phone. In some cases, the phone numbers printed on the receipt books did not exist!

This is taken by members of the community as a minor anomaly, happy to believe that it is an aberration, that most funds are put to the purpose they were collected for. After all, the members have few alternatives. If they want to give charity or zakat, there are only a handful of authentic networks in the country. So when a madrasa representative turns up, it is taken as an easy opportunity to atone for all the sins, and make an investment for akhirat—Hereafter. Almost every middle-class colony in metro-politan cities is frequented by a madrasa representative for fund collection.

There is another level at which the madrasa teachers and students are in great demand in new housing societies. Most societies have no provision for a masjid or madrasa. So, the nearest madrasa, often up to 10 kilometres or so, is contacted. A man moving into a new house, wants a Quran khwani—recitation of the complete

Quran—done. He himself is either not capable of doing it with his family, or too busy. So, a madrasa is contacted to send its teachers and students to recite the Quran. And lo, within a couple of hours, the entire Quran reading is completed by the group invited for the purpose. Once it is complete, the students and teachers are asked to stay on for a quick lunch of maybe biryani and qorma. The students who do not usually get such quality fare in their madrasa are only too happy. For them it is a feast well earned. For the family it is like outsourcing of prayer!

The madrasa group is in demand again when a member of the community passes away. Then too, some faithful believe the recitation of the entire Quran has to be completed to send the reward to the departed. Though it is not proved by any verse of the Quran, the tradition goes on. Yet again madrasa students are invited home. They huddle together as they read the chapters of the Quran. Once they are through, again a sumptuous lunch awaits them. Whether, it is housewarming or somebody departing for the other world, the madrasa students stay in demand.

This though is only periodically possible; the very nature of the invitation makes a regular connect impossible. However, a lucky teacher or two, on such occasions also, is able to make lasting bond with the members of the house where the Quran khwani takes place. He is invited to come home regularly to teach the Quran to the youngsters of the family, or in some cases, to adults too.

There are other occasions too when the madrasa students are much sought after. Like at the time of Eid ul Azha when after the sacrifice of the animal, the hide is given to a local madrasa. The madrasa, in turn, sells it to a leather merchant, making a small profit in the bargain. At a more personal level, take for instance, the time of a wedding in a small village or town. In many cases, the parents of the boy and the girl are illiterate. Hence, they cannot fill the details required for a nikahnama. So, a couple of students are called over to write down all the details, including the names of the spouses, their parents' names, temporary and permanent residences, earning, mehr, etc. Of course, at times the qazi who solemnizes the nikaah is also arranged by a local madrasa. In some cases, he could be a teacher himself!

Unknown to the larger society, maybe it does not even register with common Muslims, but madrasas, particularly the irregular, unregistered ones, touch the lives of a majority of Muslims in India, even if the Sachar Committee put the percentage of Muslims who send their children to madrasas at a mere 4 per cent!

Madrasas and Fatwas

The role of the fatwa hit mainstream Indian politics in the 1970s. Since then, in almost all General Elections, and many assembly elections, the media has wondered aloud about the fatwa from Delhi's Jama Masjid, and how it is likely to change the equations one way or the other. Back then, it was the Prime Minister Indira Gandhi against whom a call emanated from the Jama Masjid as Imam Abdullah Bukhari vowed to punish the Prime Minister for the killings of the innocent in communal riots. Then came the Emergency. Soon after, Bukhari was courted by most Opposition leaders. His fatwa, or advice, to vote for a political party, was considered the equivalent of an order to Muslims to vote accordingly. With Indira Gandhi soundly defeated in the 1977 General Elections, Bukhari's clout became enviable. In most elections since then, he (later his son Ahmed Bukhari) was cultivated by almost all political parties to gain his nod. The Bukharis proved a hard bargainer, but disappointed not a political party. If at one time, there was a call to vote for Janata Dal or the Bahujan Samaj Party, there was even a call to vote for the Bharatiya Janata Party in 2004! Maybe, it had something to do with the wider acceptability of Atal Bihari Vajpayee who had been known to have visited the imam many times after the Emergency, or the age-old animosity with the Indian National Congress. Either way, till 2019 elections, fatwa was eagerly sought and awaited from the historic Jama Masjid. Nobody asked how a fatwa could come from a masjid, how was an imam qualified to issue a fatwa, or what was the status of a fatwa. Was it an order, or a piece of advice? After all, in everyday life, is one failed to procure a desired fatwa from one qazi, he could go to another and get a fatwa suiting his argument.

These niceties mattered not a bit to our politicians or the media. The reality, however, is starkly different. An imam, even the so-called Shahi Imam of Shah Jahan's Jama Masjid, cannot issue a fatwa. He is not qualified to issue one. He has no control if one does not go by it. A fatwa can only be issued by men qualified in Islamic jurisprudence. For a long time now, some of the bigger madrasas have issued fatwas impacting the lives of the faithful without getting any media coverage. Many give in writing personally to the party. Others publish it in their monthly or quarterly journal. Still others, just attach it to a soft board visible to general public. The idea is to have maximum transparency. In fact, Darul Uloom, Deoband, has a separate department of fatwa called Darul Ifta where people send in their questions through post, email or hard copy, and seek advice. The questions range from the direction in which to pray if one is in a vehicle, supplication for growing a beard, permissibility of oral sex or otherwise, or wearing a veil or not. Most questions are about property inheritance. Not an insignificant number is about husband and wife's private relationship. Interestingly, the questions come from across the world, including places like the USA, the UK and Pakistan. The Darul Ifta with qualified Islamic scholars on board, is expected to give just the right advice keeping in mind the letter and spirit of the Quran and Hadiths. Often it does help in sorting out ticklish issues, restoring peace and order in many families through its rulings on matters of marriage, divorce, inheritance, etc. The Darul Ifta of Deoband (started in early 1890s), and indeed, countless other madrasas, to that extent guide the community on issues of religion, and help to interpret Islamic law for the common people. However, not every fatwa is according to the spirit of the Quran, or the sunnah. Often, our madrasas have ruled in a manner which makes one think if they are working in a social vacuum. For example, there was a Darul Uloom, Deoband fatwa prohibiting Muslim teenage girls from riding bicycles!

The fatwa came in 2010 and was issued by Mufti Arshad Faruqui, chairman of the Darul Ifta at that time. He sought to justify his strange ruling,

> When a grown-up girl goes cycling outside her house, it is bound to result in undue exposure…. Even medical science has given us evidence to believe that cycling is not good for adolescent girls, physically. Apart from affecting their feminity, it is harmful for their body structure.

Fortunately, either the fatwa did not reach the masses, or they chose to ignore it considering there have been no reports of Muslim girls giving up cycling after the fatwa! Incidentally, till June 2019, Darul Ifta, Deoband had issued 9,143 fatwas in English.

Or take the Deoband ruling on instant triple talaq. Not only has the Darul Ifta consistently supported instant triple talaq at a single sitting, in one of the fatwas, it even ruled a divorce valid when it was pronounced in a drunken state. The Quran puts the conditions of divorce clearly through Surah Baqarah and Surah Talaq. In the light of the two surahs, instant triple talaq is not valid, nor is a talaq pronounced in a drunken state. Divorce pronounced in a drunken state was not held valid by Muslim jurists, or even caliphs. Yet, it was considered valid by Hanafi jurists—Darul Ifta, Deoband and most madrasas base their rulings on the Hanafi texts and principles—who held that the divorce was considered valid as a way of punishment for a man who has taken to drinking! How does a divorce dissuade one from drinking was never explained. And why should a woman suffer because the man has no control over his drinking habits was not explained either.

Faruqui's was not the only avoidable fatwa. There have been many others. For instance, one where a woman was asked to wait for 90 years for her missing husband before being free to marry another man! Well-known Islamic scholar Faizur Rahman who is associated with the Chennai-based Islamic Forum for the Promotion of Moderate Thought highlighted many such anomalies in a piece for New Age Islam when he wrote, 'Deoband has also been criticised for saying that blood donation is un-Islamic on the grounds that human beings are not the "owners" of their body parts "to handle them freely."' In another fatwa, Darul Uloom cited a 7th-century safety requirement to rule that women can travel on their own only up to 48 miles. Beyond this distance they have to be accompanied by their husbands or a Mahram, that is, a person with whom marriage is illegal such as a father or brother; to say nothing about the fatwa that asked Muslim girls to go by their parents' choice on marriage for 'according to some imams, the "nikah" (marriage) of a girl who marries without the consent and permission of her guardian is "invalid."'

According to Rahman,

> One may also be astonished to know that the Hidaya (book of guidance) contains hair-splitting discussions on such improbable subjects as the validity of a divorce applied to any specific part of body such as the hand, foot, ear or nose; and partial divorce where the husband pronounces half a divorce on his wife. In the first case Hidaya rules that divorce does not take place while in the second, it is decreed that it amounts to one divorce. The explanation offered is; divorce is not capable of division and therefore, three half divorces would be equal to three divorces because each moiety amounts to one complete divorce! And there is more. What if a husband tells his wife, 'You are divorced if you enter so and so city?' According to the Hidaya, divorce takes place on her entering that city. It may be mentioned here that Hidaya is one of the books of Fiqh that is taught at Deoband.

If such fatwas bring ridicule, there are also countless other decisions arrived at through Darul Qaza or shariah courts which help many a troubled marriage. These are informal shariah courts, held valid by our legal system. Here, Muslims come for resolution of conflict in the light of the Quran and sunnah. The Darul Qaza courts provide swift and cost-effective justice, something not always possible in our legal system where the cases often take years before they are finally resolved. The Darul Qazas are often attached to madrasas in places like Maharashtra, Bihar and Madhya Pradesh, thereby increasing the values of the madrasas. Again, the madrasas were not designed or built with the shariah courts in mind. But it is an add-on role which the madrasas have been playing with aplomb.

Yes, well beyond the call of duty, or the imagined world of constant sessions of memorizing the Quran, the madrasas play a key, if underappreciated role in the life of the faithful. Of course, it works both ways. If it helps the common man get justice without too much delay, it also enhances the prestige of the madrasa and the attendant court.

For the moment though, one cannot help thinking, more Darul Qaza courts could help our over-worked judiciary by reducing the pressure on the official judicial system.

Madrasas and Freedom Struggle

Often found buried in school textbooks has been the contribution of Darul Uloom, Deoband towards India's struggle for Independence. The acknowledgement of Deoband is there. Yet it is almost self-effacing, as if the historians concerned are acknowledging the feat despite themselves. But Deoband which started as a madrasa in 1866 to spread the pristine teachings of the Quran and the Prophet played a crucial role in our freedom struggle.

At a time when the freedom struggle was in danger of being divided along the lines of religion—the Hindu Mahasabha, and later the RSS were steadfastly pro-British, their primary enemies being the Muslims while the Muslim League from the late 1930s wanted a separate country for Muslims—the Deoband movement not only brought Indian Muslims into the freedom struggle in huge numbers, it also built a bridge between the two major communities. For Deoband, the struggle was all about preserving the idea of India, rather than safeguarding community-specific interests. If India survived, the communities could arrive at an amicable understanding in due course. For the moment, Hindus and Muslims must unite to get rid of the British.

As stated by noted freedom fighter and Parliamentarian Maulana Syed Asad Madani in his concluding address in Rajya Sabha,

> They (Maulana Mahmood Hasan and Maulana Hussain Ahmad Madani) realised the need for Hindu–Muslim joint platform and joint leadership for spearheading the freedom movement. They were also convinced that India can never attain independence without forging a joint alliance of Hindus and Muslims. Therefore, they persuaded the Indian National Congress to spearhead the freedom movement under the leadership of Gandhiji. Maulana Abdulbari Firangi Mahali, in the very presence of Maulana Mahmood Hasan issued a declaration that, from that day onwards, Gandhiji will be called Mahatma Gandhi. After that, freedom movement gained further momentum. The freedom of India owes much to the great sacrifices made by the likes of Maulana Mahmood Hasan and his companions, Maulana Abul Kalam Azad, Khan Abdul Ghaffar Khan, Dr Ansari, Hakim Ajmal Khan, Maulana Mohammad Ali Jauhar, Maulana Obaidullah Sindhi, Maulana Hussain Ahmad Madani, etc. In fact, they were torchbearers of freedom movement who raised the banner of revolt against the British in 1936.

As for Madani's call, in 1919 Mahatma Gandhi was spearheading a non-violent struggle against colonial masters. With the Rowlatt Act and Jallianwala Bagh massacre eroding the faith of the Moderates and worsening the relations between India and Britain, Mahatma Gandhi sensed an opportunity to widen the social base of the struggle. As Deoband and Jamiat leaders suggested, he took up the cause of restoration of the Caliphate, something which was close to Muslim conscience. At this time, Deoband through Jamiat Ulama-e-Hind gave him whole-hearted support, thus widening the social base of the freedom struggle. It gave the movement an entirely different dimension. Now the Congress had the open support of the best-known Muslim body. Deoband, like, Firangi Mahal in Lucknow, was steadfastly anti-British.

From hereon, the role of Deoband became increasingly important in our freedom struggle. It was a body of nationalists who stood up not only to the British, but also acted as a perfect foil to Muslim League's designs for a separate state of Pakistan. Important leaders of Jamiat Ulama-e-Hind had a direct lineage with Deoband. Like Maulvi Mohiuddin fought the British in Kerala, Maulvi Kifayatullah, Mohammed Miyan and Husain Ahmed Madani played a significant role in the freedom struggle in the 1920s and 1930s. Incidentally, in 1937 there was a direct debate between Madani and Mohammad Iqbal, the former standing for India's composite nationalism, the latter for the idea of the Muslim state of Pakistan. Thanks to Deoband's scholars, Muslim League could not garner the support of most Muslims.

In fact, today, many Deobandi scholars boast that they were the first ones to raise a cry for Independence from the British. They refer to Maulana Mahmood Hasan, popularly known as Shaikhul Hind (1851–1920), who had organized a plan to overthrow the British. Hasan though planned to wage a jihad to oust the British for restoring the perceived Muslim government. Hasan did not limit himself to India in his endeavour. He looked for help from Muslim countries. It was when he was on a mission to collect arms that he got arrested in 1916. The British sent him and his companions to Malta where they were kept under detention for three years. Incidentally, Hasan was among the foremost students of Darul Uloom Deoband. He was the best-known disciple of Maulana Qasim Nanautawi, the founder of Deoband.

As stated by Madani in 'Parliamentary Speeches of Maulana Syed Asad Madani' (translated from Urdu by Mohammad Anwer Hussain and Sayeed Suhrawardy; published by Manak Publications),

In 1803, the East India Company issued a proclamation that all the subjects belong to God, country to the Emperor and rule of the Company Bahadur. Shah Abdul Aziz (1746–1824), a leading scholar of his time and son of Shah Waliullah Dehlawi (1703–1762) issued the famous fatwa in 1803 declaring that India had ceased to be a Darul Islam. This fatwa was a landmark in the history of India in general and Muslims in particular. It amounted to a call to religious conscientious Muslims to mobilise them in the absence of a powerful Muslim ruler, under whose popular leadership they would rise in defence against a foreign power. Words of this fatwa still reverberate in our ears that sparked first war of Independence in 1857. The mighty British, to some extent, suppressed the movement led by Shah Abdul Aziz, but the fire he lit in 1857 took the shape of raging fire against the British Government, when Maulana Mahmood Hasan adopted the anti-British mantle and sent his disciples to Afghanistan for launching jihad against the British regime. They were first to establish independent government in Afghanistan and appointed Raja Mahender Pratap as the first President.

It was, however, not the first foray of Hasan towards elimination of the colonial rule. Back in 1878, he had formed Samratut Tarbiah. The body reappeared in a new form in the form of Jamiatul Ansar in 1909. Its first session was held in 1911 in Moradabad. The session was presided over by Ahmad Hasan Amrohawi who said, 'The movement of Jamiatul Ansar had begun almost 30 years ago. The founders of this movement were the students of Madrasa Alia. The movement suffered a setback because it could not adjust itself to the needs of the time.' Then there was the establishment of Nizaratul Maarif or the Academy of Quranic Learning whose spiritual guide was once again Hasan. Its main purpose was to overthrow the British. As written by Maulana Hussain Ahmad Madani,

The purpose behind establishing Nizaratul Maarif was to make Muslim youth stronger believers, and to instruct and guide them, specially western-educated Muslims, in the Quranic teachings in such a logical way that it would remove the poisonous impact of anti-Islam propaganda and ill-founded scepticism about practicality of Islamic belief and tenets in modern age.

The British understood the purpose of such a body. The findings of a research conducted by the Central Intelligence Department of the British government, said, 'Maulana Obaidullah Sindhi could not use Darul Uloom Deoband as a training camp for his missionaries (Mujahideen). He, therefore, decided to establish a Madrasa (Nizaratul Maarif) in Delhi to achieve this purpose.'

However, In *The Prisoners of Malta: The Heart-Rending Tale of Muslim Freedom Fighters in British Period* (written by Maulana Syed Mohammed Mian and translated by Mohammed Anwer Hussain and Hasan Imam, published by Manak), it is said, 'It would be more appropriate to call Nizaratul Maarif a nursing home where the sentimentally injured freedom fighters used to gather and share feelings of those who were calling upon people to unite and stand against the oppressive British regime.'

Seek knowledge from cradle to grave, and search for it even if you have to go to China.

—PROPHET MUHAMMAD (PBUH)

MADRASAS IN DYSTOPIA

Imam Hafiz Salim
Baraut, Uttar Pradesh

Imam Hafiz Mohammed Salim speaks without a note of rancour. Yet, every sentence of his tells you of the sense of denial he nurses some 30 years after he left Madrasa Ashraful in Muzaffarnagar.

'We were around 100 residential students. There were 200 day scholars too. There were 10–12 teachers. The students were normally taught hifz–memorizing the Quran. Those who pursued higher education were taught Arabic and Persian. In Arabic, grammar was also taught. The students who were studying to be hafiz never learnt Arabic; only those who wanted to be alim or maulvi stayed back to learn the language. The hifz boys memorized the Quran in three to four years and left the madrasa. Usually, they went out to find themselves a job at another madrasa or a masjid. Some became an imam, some settled for being a muezzin. The madrasa itself did not have any placement facility unless some masjid in the vicinity put in a request. Every year 15–20 boys became hafiz. Today, when a boy becomes a hafiz and goes back to his village, he can hope to earn ₹5000 or ₹6000.'

Salim, now blessed with a robust frame, piercing eyes and a luxuriant beard, did not start his academic pursuit in Muzaffarnagar. He, like most children of his neighbourhood, went to the madrasa in his village.

'I studied for four years in my village. The madrasa was Sirajul Uloom. It is in Idrispur village in district Baghpat. We had three teachers and around 100 students. My father admitted all his children to a madrasa. He did not send anybody to a private school. I am the eldest of six brothers and sisters. All the three brothers are hafiz. The sisters stopped going to madrasa after they had learnt to read the Quran. The brothers stayed on for about four years to become hafiz.'

Why did the sisters drop out?

'I cannot say. They should have continued, but I guess it is the social tradition in the village. It is considered enough for a girl to be able to read the Quran, and maybe write her name and address. If a girl becomes a hafiz, they say, it becomes difficult to get a suitable groom.'

From the madrasa in his village, he joined the bigger madrasa in Muzaffarnagar. Shockingly, neither madrasa was recognized.

'Yes, it is true. No madrasa was recognized then, or even now. The madrasas enjoyed zero Government support and survived almost fully on local people's charity. The village madrasa ran on the locals' contributions; some farmers gave cereals. The cereals in turn were sold in the market to pay the salary of the teachers, and meet sundry expenses of the madrasa. The Muzaffarnagar madrasa had a proper receipt book for people's contributions. But let me tell you, the contributions were hardly sufficient. The students slept on the floor. There were no rugs, no fans, no coolers. In winters too, we all slept on the bare floor or at best with a rug spread on it. Some students arranged for a charpoy, most slept on a rug and shared blankets which they would have brought from home. The madrasa provided two square meals. No fruits were provided, no milk or Bournvita. Two meals and plain water. That is all. In winter too the students bathed with cold water as there were no heaters or geysers. At times, the students had to run errands for their teachers. It was common for students to wash the clothes of their teachers, press their feet, and do sundry other jobs like getting a paan from a neighbourhood stall. The madrasa teachers are not skilful or very well read. They would have studied in a similar madrasa. Hence, they would not have been particularly well equipped. Even today, their salary ranges from ₹6 to ₹10,000. In rare cases, it goes up to ₹13000. Also, back in our times, the students, particularly hifz students were given physical punishment. Now, at least things are better. I know of a madrasa where the erring students are asked to offer certain rakaat (cycles) of salaat (prayer) when they make a mistake.'

Yet it was not all gloom and doom.

'Though the madrasas never arranged picnic or inter-madrasa competitions, the boys used to arrange these matches themselves. Football or volleyball matches were popular. Cricket would have been too costly for them with bat, ball, wickets, pads and everything. Life was simple. Money was limited. Also, we never had to go out to purchase books. They came from Deoband and were all provided by the madrasa free of cost. Today, I cannot recall their authors, but I did learn Arabic grammar in my madrasa as I pursued my alim course. It helped me understand Quranic Arabic too. We were taught Farsi (Persian) also as there are words of Farsi in Arabic. As the madrasa had no affiliation, some teachers on their own initiative taught us basic English, Hindi and maths. But there were no computers. For these languages, a student had to show some initiative on his own, and he was given one hour every day to learn these subjects. Otherwise, for four hours in the morning, and another two–three hours in the afternoon, we only studied the Quran, memorized it, learnt a bit of Arabic, etc.'

In all, Salim put in around eight years in his madrasa education. Today, he rues that the certificates he worked so hard for are not recognized anywhere. The AMU, Jamia Millia Islamia and Maulana Azad National Urdu University which either keep some seats for madrasa students in certain streams or actively encourage madrasa students to pursue higher, secular education, do not recognize certificates from countless such madrasas.

'The certificate from the madrasa is not recognized anywhere. It is just useful for word of mouth acknowledgement in the locality. You gain social points in the neighbourhood. That is all. You cannot go to AMU or Jamia with this certificate. The universities also do not recognize such a certificate. Yet the madrasas do not opt for recognition. It is a bizarre condition. There are some students from well off families in villages who come here while most are poor. Yet nobody pays attention to the fact that the madrasa certificate will not help in earning a livelihood. The rich have the option of going back to family business, the poor have nowhere to go. But the madrasas should try to help the families tide over poverty do nothing to help their economic condition.'

Imam Salim studied at a small madrasa in his village before going to Baraut

Under the circumstances, the move of the governments in states like Maharashtra, Uttar Pradesh and Rajasthan asking the students to teach secular subjects besides theological ones, to gain recognition from the Central Board of Secondary Education, should be well received. The madrasas though consider it 'madakhalat' (interference). Salim differs,

'Any intervention of the Government in this matter can only be positive. The Quran asks us to pursue knowledge, all knowledge that is beneficial to mankind has to be followed. Not just knowledge of Farsi or Arabic. Today, even though many madrasas have started keeping a teacher for English or Hindi, the efforts at best are elementary. A lot more needs to be done.'

So, will he send his son to his madrasa? Or maybe some other one?

'No way. He is my son. I will not recommend to anybody else either.'

Not surprisingly, when Salim's first son was born he got him admitted to an English medium school in Ghaziabad—Salim himself was an imam at a local mosque then. By the time, he was blessed with another son and a daughter a little later, he had moved to Noida to be the imam at another mosque which gave him one-room 'family accommodation'. He preferred to send his children to co-educational public schools in the satellite township instead of sending them down to the madrasa run at the mosque. Reason?

'Most madrasas confine themselves to giving knowledge of the Hereafter. They instil knowledge about religion, but in their quest for Afterlife, they forget this life. This madrasa here is no different. As a joke goes, the madrasas confine themselves to what is beyond the skies and below the earth, not having anything to do with what goes on on this earth!'

. . .

The Quran lays a lot of stress on learning. Every human being is supposed to pursue ilm or knowledge. There is no gender bias there, the instruction is as applicable to men as women. In fact, there is an oft-quoted saying of the Prophet wherein he is reported to have said, 'For pursuing education, go as far as China'. The 7th century Arabia when the Prophet is said to have given this advice was by no means amenable to travel. The desert landscape was harsh, the weather challenging and the means of transport elementary at best. China then, could as well, be as far as the moon. Yet, the Prophet asked his followers to pursue knowledge even if they had to travel to China. Significantly, for him ilm was not only about religion, but also anything that could make life better for humanity. Thus included was the knowledge of maths and science, algebra and astronomy, philosophy and jurisprudence, etc. There was no vertical split of the religious and the secular.

Understandably, Islam laid a lot of stress on ilm, knowledge. Soon enough, the madrasas started as centres of uloom, the plural of ilm. Initially, there were no separate madrasas and mosques served as centres of dissemination of knowledge. Men, women and children all pursued knowledge. There is a well-known incident from the Prophet's life where he is said to have once entered al Masjid-al Nabavi in a leisure hour, and was pleasantly surprised to find two groups of people engrossed in study in separate batches. While one group was reciting and memorizing the Quran, the other was discussing the subjects mentioned in the book; the Prophet preferred the latter. That was probably one of the earliest instances of a debating society in Islam, also one of a madrasa where you were allowed to learn, revise, explore, discuss, debate and question.

The madrasas today, however, are essentially Islamic schools where the Quran and Hadith are taught. Like an engineering or a medical college is supposed to churn out engineers or doctors, the madrasas are supposed to provide moral and spiritual leadership to the community in particular, and the society in general. There is an unfortunate vertical divide in education, secular and sacred. The madrasas are supposed to provide a class of scholars or ulemma who can interpret Islam. In fact, often in madrasas, youngsters are told they are being groomed to take over as the leaders in tomorrow's world. It, of course, does not work out that way. The fault is not of the fresh madrasa graduates but in the madrasa system of education. It is a system caught in a time warp where the core syllabus has not been changed for hundreds of years; only artificial and lopsided additions of secular learning made.

Some scholars believe the syllabus was initially framed in the 17th century, and was then revised in 1750s, about half a century after the last of the great Mughals Aurangzeb breathed his lasting 1707. Others point out to the fact that till the victory of the British in the First War of Independence in 1857, the madrasas were central to the life of people. They imparted holistic education without any vertical split of the religious and the secular. That division was introduced by the British who, in their overweening ignorance believed, madrasas were not equipped to impart lessons of science. They were helped by those Indians who believed people had gone astray by studying general sciences, geography, mathematics, English, etc. They wanted Muslims to go back to a presumed golden age when madrasas only prepared the faithful for the world's spiritual leadership. At the same time, the British were not ready to touch a religious form of learning for fear of hurting the locals' sentiments. Thus came about schools that provided learning of subjects like English, mathematics, geography, physics and biology. The madrasas were confined to religious learning. They have not emerged fully from this watertight segregation introduced in the second half of the 19th century. Of course, there was another motive behind the division of the sacred and the secular: an alim of Islam would not know much about the ways of the world, hence would not be able to guide the community. The scholars of the secular world would not know much about Islam; hence will not be able to contribute to a wider study of faith. Deen and duniya (faith and the world) became mutually opposed.

Once the pivot of the Muslim world, madrasas today are marginalized within the Muslim community. The well-off, the well-read, the well-placed Muslims do not send their children to madrasas anymore. The non-Muslims stopped doing so almost 70 years ago except in the states of Kerala and Bengal where the madrasas continue to fulfil their initial purpose of providing education without vertical barriers of the sacred and the mundane. It did not happen overnight. The process was gradual, painful, self-defeating. At the time of the Prophet, the faithful were one community. And learning, whether theological or secular, was appreciated as long as it was beneficial for mankind. Thanks to such a mindset, the ummah gave luminaries like Ibn Sina and Ibn Rushd, etc. Things began to change after the last of the caliphs, Ali, bade goodbye to the world. The community began to be divided into sects. The first major sect was the Shiite. Then, with each imam, there came about a new set of followers who called themselves Muslim, but often laid much greater stock on the teachings of their particular imam than the teachings of the Prophet. Thus Muslims came to be Hanafis, Malikis, Shafi'is, Hanbalis, etc., and ceased to be just Muslims. Amidst myriad interpretations and trenchant criticism was the simple teaching of the Quran as told through Surah Maida, verse 3, 'This day, I have perfected for you your religion and completed My favour upon you.'

In India, though Islam came at the time of the Prophet with the establishment of the first mosque in India, Cheraman Jummah Masjid in Thrissur district, it needed the establishment of the Delhi Sultanate in 1206 for the religion to have a firm footing. The madrasas as centres of learning started evolving during the 13th century, but really came into their own only with the coming of the Mughals. The Mughals were Hanafis, so most Muslims are Hanafis in India, at least from the early 16th century. The Hanafis are said to be among the more conservative sects. Today, the madrasa system of education in India is based on the Hanafi curriculum called Dars-e-Nizami. It was prepared by Mullah Nizamuddin of Firangi Mahal, Lucknow. The Mullah was patronized by the last of the great Mughals, Aurangzeb. Be it as the Darul Uloom Deoband with its world fame, or the much smaller sundry madrasas with some 50 students and two teachers in Telengana, Bihar and Haryana, Dars-e-Nizami is followed in almost every madrasa. The students at these madrasas study, as Islamic scholar Faizur Rahman wrote in a perceptive article, *Deoband: The Face of Hanafism in India* (NewAgeIslam) classical texts of the Hanafi schools.

Insofar as religious Fiqh (law) is concerned, students undergoing the eight-year course at Deoband study the following books: Noorul Izah, Qudoori, Sharah Wiqayah and Hidaya. One does not have to be exceptionally perceptive to guess that all the four books are classical texts of Hanafi fiqh.

Even the compendiums on principles of jurisprudence (Usool al-Fiqh) that form part of the syllabus, such as Tasheelul Usool, Usool as Shasi, Alfauzul Kabeer, Husamy, Manahilul Irfan and Musallemus saboot, are Hanafi works. In other words, a graduate of Deoband, who will enjoy the privilege of being called an aalim (an Islamic scholar) after completing the marathon eight-year course, would know very little on Islamic jurisprudence beyond the Hanafi point of view.

Since Deoband is the fountainhead or inspiration for thousands of madrasas across North India (the influence of Jamaat-e-Islami Hind is relatively muted in much of North and Central India, and more pronounced in the South), the smaller madrasas too follow the same template. As Hafiz Mohammed Salim, a business-man who was an imam for more than a decade, says, 'The books at our madrasa were provided free. Whenever any student lost the book or it got torn, a new one was procured from Deoband. The books were available locally only at select shops which got them from Deoband.'

It springs no surprise that almost all these madrasas follow the Hanafi texts, and seek to emulate Deoband in their syllabus fully. It is something which has not gone down well with students who have passed out of madrasas and discovered that their learn-ing far from equipping them to be the moral leaders of the world, does not prepare them to be scholars of Islam who can debate about the facets of each sect, be it Wahabis, Ahl-e-Hadith, Barelvi, Deobandi, etc. Worse, they have no idea of comparative religion, and when they are called upon to decide emerging issues of a pluralist society, they are found wanting. They have no clue about Hinduism, Christianity, Sikhism or even the ways of Islam beyond the subcontinent. As Naseem-ur-Rahman, a madrasa graduate from Jamiat ul Falah madrasa in Azamgarh, said in an interview (*Communalism Combat*, September 2004),

> Many madrasas place an inordinate stress on the nitty-gritty of fiqh (jurisprudence). I am not saying that fiqh is not important, but that much of what the madrasas teach in fiqh

is simply irrelevant, and outdated. For instance, the old fiqh books that continue to be used in most madrasas discuss in great detail such issues as: What should you do to purify a well if a cat or a lizard falls inside it? How much water should you remove from the well in order to restore its purity? Is it legal to eat a bird that has been shot while flying? And so on.

It is a point Faizur Rahman too made in his article. He wrote in 2015, 'Scholar Waris Mazhari, a graduate of the Deoband madrasa, is severely critical of the curriculum of his alma mater.' He thinks, 'The syllabus is irrelevant and unable to meet the challenges of modern life' because of its outdated texts. He cites the example of Shara -i- Aqa'id, the 600-year-old theological treatise, taught in the seventh year at Deoband, and says that its archaic style, full of references to antiquated Greek philosophy, is beyond the understanding of students. It deals with 'imaginary and hypothetical problems and verbal puzzles' such as the questions: 'Is there one sky or seven or nine? Or, can the sky be broken into parts?', and therefore, books such as Shara-i-Aqa'id, which are no longer taught in the schools in the Arab world, should be removed at once from the syllabus, although many conservative Ulema at Deoband would vehemently disagree. In the opinion of Mazhari, what madrasas need today 'are books of theology that also take into account the confirmed findings of modern science.'

Even as future scholars are groomed for hypothetical battles of cleaning a well after a lizard falls into it, the madrasas do not equip them to face the emerging issues of modern-day life. For instance, the students are not taught about the status of organ transplant in Islam. Or about cloning. Even everyday problems faced by the Muslim community, like insurance for house or vehicle or interest—driven loans for home, education or medical treatment, are not given the attention they deserve. Not that there are no relevant books on the subject. Many scholars like Maulana Wahiduddin Khan, Abdullah Tariq and Yusuf Islahi, etc., have written extensively on the subject, but the madrasas fail to prescribe these books of *jadeed fiqhi masail* or issues of contemporary relevance. One of the possible reasons for exclusion of such books is that they may not necessarily be of the same sect as the madrasa or its proprietors. Thus the students lose out due to the sectarian divisions between the ulemma. Under the circumstances, the Quran ought to have been the glue to bind the ummah together, and all issues sorted out in the light of the Quran. Yet, shockingly, it does not happen that way simply because the Quran is regarded only as a book of reverence, and placed accordingly. It is not regarded as a book of life, one that would give guidance for all challenges. Hence, the students are supposed to memorize it, accumulate points for the Hereafter for their exertions, but not study it to find answers to the questions that might crop up in the mind. Nor can they consult their teachers at the madrasa simply because they too, having studied in a similar madrasa, would not be equipped to provide informed answers. The Quran repeatedly asks the believers to explore the world, introspect, ask questions. The madrasas, to the contrary, revel in their rote learning methods. The Quran is reduced to a book that is memorized by students in the initial years in a madrasa, kissed, touched with the forehead and put back in a velvet cover after every reading. Never is a student encouraged to ask questions about it, or seek answers through it. At Deoband, in the first five years of study only its translation (Tarjumatul Quran) and short exegesis are taught. In the sixth year, the 15th century commentary Tafsir-e-Jalalayn is introduced along with some books on the principles of exegesis and jurisprudence. Quranic study is given a break in the seventh and eighth year but makes a comeback in the post-graduation classes under the head Mastery in Tafsir. Here again students get to learn only portions of the 13th and 14th century exegeses Baizaawi and Tafsir ibn Kaseer respectively.

If any further proof is needed to establish that madrasas are caught in a time warp, it comes from the inclusion of the commentary of Ibn Kathir for the students. Ibn Kathir was an early 14th century scholar of Islam, who wrote a famous commentary of the Quran called Tafseer al Quran al Azeem which links certain sayings of the Prophet to the verses of the Quran. Though regarded with great respect in madrasa circles, the book does not have universal approval with many of the scholars terming it a 'philological work' and finding it 'very elementary'. Yet our madrasa students are not taught the tafseer or 20th or 21st century scholars like Sheikh Abubakr Gumi or Taqi Usmani, Tariq Jameel, Israr Ahmed or Sheikh Qazi Sanaullah Panipati, etc. Of course, it is not even considered to introduce the youngsters to scholars like Yasir Qadhi, Noman Ali Khan, Bilal Philips or A. R. Green who have carved out quite a following thanks to their online lectures and live classes. A woman scholar like Farhat Hashmi is a strict no-no. Incidentally, when Hashmi first made waves in India about a decade ago, some of the clerics advised the faithful to stay away from her classes as Hashmi being a woman, was only supposed to look after her house and family. She could, at best, according to them, give right grooming to her own children. She had to have awaz ka purdah (voice veil of sorts wherein a woman is not heard by men other than those in her family) with rest of the world.

Due to this constant fascination for looking at the supposed past, the madrasas have neither changed their syllabus to meet emerging challenges, nor prepared their scholars to work in a multi-religious society or multi-sect Muslim world. The Hanafi madrasas provide their core text books, the Ahl-e-Hadith do likewise. Worse, the students are not encouraged to know about other religions, or even other sects. As Naseemur Rahman said,

> Madrasas are meant to train a class of religious scholars or ulemma who can interpret and preach Islam. Now, it is for the community to decide how far the madrasas in the country, which numbers in the thousands, are actually achieving this. In order for the ulemma to provide proper guidance to the community, they must know about what is happening in the world outside the four walls of their madrasas. In many madrasas, the teachers and managers forbid their students to even read books and magazines published by other Muslim groups, let alone by non-Muslims. Naturally, this works to greatly narrow their vision and severely limit their understanding of the rapidly changing world around them.

In turn, this only makes them appear as awkward aliens once they graduate from the madrasas and are forced to confront the outside world. In the madrasas, teachers constantly tell their students that they are being groomed to become leaders of the community, arguing that the right to leadership, rests with them. Imagine the shock these students receive once they finish their studies and suddenly discover that no one wants to accept their leadership claims, and, even worse, when they realise that they are regarded as irrelevant as they cannot relate to the wider society.

The madrasas, which are reduced to places of religious learning, have actually reshaped the discourse of education. Far from providing lawyers and judges, doctors and engineers well versed with Islamic tenets, they provide only students who memorized the Quran, or who can, at best, argue on matters of fiqh, books that ceased to have direct relevance in the life of the faithful with the decline of the Mughals. The madrasas in India are caught in a dystopia, religious institutions whose products once acted as civil servants of the society, are today merely imagined moral guardians.

To listen to the instructions of sciences and learning for one hour is more meritorious than attending the funerals of a thousand martyrs, and more meritorious than standing up in prayer for a thousand nights.

—PROPHET MUHAMMAD (PBUH)

Chapter 9

THE NEED FOR MODERNIZATION

Ahmed Laisi
Madrasa Riyazul Uloom, Delhi

Some 27 years after he passed out of a madrasa with a fazilat degree, Prof Ahmed Laisi remains a picture of gratitude and modesty. Having spent a good part of his life within the precincts of madrasas, life, for him, is a prayer. Everything has to be done with care and devotion; be it his family trying to find stability in Delhi, or Laisi himself trying to keep his career on an even keel in Hyderabad. Just back from Isha prayers after a long, challenging day, Laisi who is now an academic with Maulana Azad National Urdu University in Hyderabad, teaching medieval history, remembers his madrasa days like he left it just yesterday.

'For seven years I studied at Madrasa Jamia Sirajul Uloom in Ghonda district of Uttar Pradesh. It was an Ahl-e-Hadith madrasa. Then I came to Riyazul Uloom in Delhi. I did my faziliat from there. There were a couple of reasons for coming here. First, Riyazul Uloom has a certain dignity and respect attached to its name. Second, its certificates and degrees are recognized by Central universities. I did not want to confine myself to madrasa education and wanted to pursue higher learning at a university. So, I joined here for fazilat course. I got all cooperation for my other studies from the madrasa. While in Riyazul Uloom I did my computer course from a private institute in Okhla in South-East Delhi. For the three months course, I used to go to Okhla every day. My madrasa authorities did not object. In fact, the madrasa did not object if you sought private tuition or sought a university degree. It is one of the best things about it. One is able to pursue traditional learning and also study for a job. For me one of the reasons that attracted me here was its certificates and degrees were acknowledged in central universities. I studied here for a year. I even studied briefly at Madrasa Hussain Bux which is near Jama Masjid. I did a paper of Mishkar Sharief from there. Among my teachers there was Mullah Noor. I was not fortunate to study under the well-known alim Akhlaq Husain Qasmi Sahab, but I met him later. I interviewed him many years later when I was working with the Election Commission.'

Having spent his time balancing his fazilat degree with computer education, Laisi was keen to widen his horizons.

'After finishing my studies at Riyazul Uloom in 1992, I wanted to join Jamia Millia Islamia which had by then announced that was acknowledging madrasa qualification. However, due to procedural delay I could get admission in History Honours in Jamia Millia Islamia only in 1994 though I had done fazilat two years earlier.'

The delay did not dampen his enthusiasm for learning. Laisi did Masters in history from the university. He followed it up with M.Phil and finally PhD in 'Analytical Study of Important Arabic Sources about Indian History during 14th century'. At that time Arabic was taught in madrasa. History was not much taught but there were plenty of books on various sects. Delhi used to have great madrasas like 'Madrasa Firozia and Madrasa Nasiriya.'

Among those who taught him at Jamia were noted academics Mujeeb Asraf and Jamaluddin. Not to forget the world-renowned Prof Mushirul Hasan. 'When I was doing M Phil, he had become the Vice-Chancellor. He did not have much time to spare, but he did teach us research methodology.'

Logically, he should have just gone on to teach at a university. Or started a madrasa in a small town to teach the next generation, and maybe groom them to step beyond the madrasas. But Laisi's life journey has been unusual from the beginning—born in a village of Domariyaganj district in eastern Uttar Pradesh, he did his basic education from a private school in Darbhanga. He finished his VIIIth standard from there before joining the madrasas in Ghonda and Delhi, two of them (Madrasa Jamia Sirajul Uloom and Riyazul Uloom) were of Ahl-e-Hadith sect, one (Madrasa Hussain Bux) was Hanafi, owing allegiance to Deoband. Nothing deterred him. Rather than feeling uncomfortable studying alongside students from different sects, Laisi realized there was space for all in madrasas. One could agree to disagree, but one had to make allocation for a differing viewpoint.

With varied education came varied private jobs. For a few years, he changed jobs frequently in the private sector. None could satisfy him until he landed a job with the Election Commission of India where he was a private secretary to the 17th Chief Election Commissioner S. Y. Quraishi who succeeded Navin Chawla in 2010. Today, he teaches at MANUU in Hyderabad but cherishes his association with madrasas.

However, rather than be just nostalgic about the years spent in madrasas, the distance in time has enabled him to take a good long, dispassionate look at the way the madrasas function, the windows they open, the doors they close.

'I understand there are madrasas which do not say anything positive about other madrasas or sects. They do not teach books of other sects. Some do not even admit students from other sects, but I have been fortunate. Wherever I have studied, I have not encountered this exclusion. At Riyazul Uloom which is an Ahl-e-Hadith madrasa, our rector Abdur Rashid Azhari used to welcome students from all faiths. If a Hanafi student would come, he would first give him admission. His idea was that a student from another sect should not feel excluded or discriminated against. We used to have both teachers and students who were Hanafis. In fact, some of the talk on differences among madrasas is exaggerated. At Deoband too they welcome all sects. I have never seen any student being sent back because he belonged to a non-Hanafi sect.'

'It has been a long journey from Domariyaganj and Darbangha to Ghonda, Delhi, and finally, Hyderabad. Not surprisingly, Laisi who had to live away from his family for long years in order to pursue education, has his son studying at a public school in New Delhi while he seeks to mould the future of students in Hyderabad! What can one do? I cannot disturb my children's education for the sake of the family being together. Today, my four kids stay in Delhi with my wife. I stay separately in Hyderabad. I meet them whenever I get a chance.'

Ahmad Khan Laisi studied at Riyazul Uloom.
He teaches History at Maulana Azad National Urdu
University in Hyderabad

. . .

In the early years after Independence, madrasas slipped under the radar. The larger secular society did not know much about the goings-on within the four walls of the Islamic seminaries. The calls as well as efforts to introduce contemporary subjects in madrasas became both audible and noticeable in 1970s. The stark contrast visible among madrasa graduates and University graduates prompted concerned persons from amongst Muslims as well as non-Muslims to do something to remove this disparity.

For obvious reasons, non-Muslims used caution in advocating the need for change. Amongst Muslims, mainly educationists shared their concern and suggestions. Initially there was a general knee-jerk rejection from most madrasas as they considered it as an interference in 'religious' affairs by non-religious Muslims, who were even labelled as government agents out to weaken Islam and its 'forts'—it may be recalled that in the 19th and early 20th centuries, madrasas were regarded as the forts of Islam by the ulemma. However, soon they realized themselves the fast pace of changes happening around, 'knowledge explosion' was too fast, too loud to be ignored. Many individuals as well as institutions made sincere efforts to bridge this gap and initiated a process of infusion which continues till date.

The Government of India also took note of the situation and a 'Modernization of Madrasa' programme started in 1993. Those madrasas which were willing to introduce modern subjects, particularly Science and Mathematics, in their curricula were given financial assistance. The National Monitory Committee for Minorities Education was constituted in 2004 to look into all aspects of education of minorities and suggest ways and means to improve the conditions for educational empowerment of minorities. Based on the recommendations of experts, a 'Scheme for Providing Quality Education in Madrasas' was introduced in 2006. To streamline the process, it was suggested to create State Madrasa Boards. As expected the response was mixed. A majority of madrasas opposed the move. However, some states did succeed in establishing the Madrasa Boards. Madhya Pradesh was among the pioneers as it established the Board in late 1990s and even introduced computers in madrasas.

Still many states do not have Madrasa Boards while other states like Bihar, Uttar Pradesh and Bengal which otherwise lag in various human indices have active Madrasa Boards. National Commission of Minority Educational Institutions suggested the creation of a Central Madrasa Board on the lines of CBSE for effective implementation of government schemes and to ensure that assistance for introduction of modern subjects is given to purely religious madrasas. Though government tried to develop a consensus on the issue, it was ultimately shelved for want of support from religious groups.

Besides these efforts at governmental level, there was an increasing realization within the community at large and stake holders in particular to catch up with changing times and trends. During the last more than two decades the authors visited scores of madrasas across the country as a part of a mission to develop a holistic system of education shunning the prevalent bifurcation of Religious (Deeni) and Worldly (Dunyavi) education and to re-establish that pursuit of knowledge and exploration of Nature for the benefit of humanity is a part of mandatory religious responsibility in Islam. At almost all places people were willing to introduce modern subjects but lacked funds and infrastructure for the same. Being uneducated they either do not know of government schemes or are not capable of doing the necessary paper work. Besides, most of the madrasas and maktabs are not run in an organized manner. There is no proper registered society to run them and to maintain proper accounting of income and expenditure as per government regulations.

However, the continuous debate about modernization has motivated many madrasas to enroll their students with NIOS and to make some arrangement or allow them to join some coaching classes to clear their high or secondary school exam.

Kadapa is a small city in Rayalaseema region of Andhra Pradesh, about 430 kms from Hyderabad. In February 2019, Kadapa Islamic Welfare Society organized a seminar in collaboration with Islamic Fiqh (Jurisprudence) Academy. The theme of this national seminar was 'Inclusion of Modern Education in Madrasas and Religious Education in Modern Educational Institutions'. Co-author (Dr Parvaiz) was invited to deliver the key-note address. During the two-day seminar, most of the speakers, who were drawn from different parts of the country, spoke favourably for madrasa enrichment. There were some apprehensions also, which were addressed during interventions or presidential remarks.

One scholar raised a basic question that just around 4 per cent of Muslim children go to madrasas. Even if they do not get the modern education people should focus on the remaining majority which does not attend any school or are not getting good schooling. This is a perception in a section of our religious scholars that unnecessarily or due to some motivated designs, scholars are after madrasas pressing for reforms.

In the concluding remarks, the co-author addressed this issue. The ritualistic religious prayers in all mosques are performed by Imams who are graduates of madrasas. Their assistants, usually called 'muezzin' are also madrasa graduates. The Imams address Friday prayer gatherings and handle other issues of the locality also. All of these Imams, 100 per cent of them are from madrasas (which attract only 4 per cent of Muslim children!) If these madrasas do not impart any modern education to these students, it is obvious they will be unaware of contemporary issues, problems or challenges facing humanity. How one can expect such people to give contemporary guidance to people. Their Friday sermons or addresses on other religious occasions are found wanting as far as contemporary issues are concerned. It is a sad story of a great opportunity lost or underutilized. One's personality is manifestation of all inputs one gets and if one gets exposure to such discourses which are entrenched in outdated issues and commentaries, the result is not difficult to comprehend. This is what is happening with large section of Muslims populace, particularly in north India. This needs to be addressed to help ameliorate the plight of this second largest part of our citizens.

The recommendations approved by consensus at the end of the seminar are suggestive of the change, settling amongst religious scholars also. Almost all the madrasas follow a curriculum called 'Dars-e-Nizami' which is of eight-year duration. When a fresh student joins madrasa and if he is totally illiterate, he/she is admitted to 'Idadia', sort of a preschool where the new entrant is kept for one to two years, as this duration varies from madrasa to madrasa. During this period the student is taught the Quran, Arabic, Urdu and some basis theology (Deeniat). The seminar recommended that during this period the students will be taught standard first to fourth curriculum of school system. From first year of madrasa course to fifth year, the student will be prepared for tenth class exam of NIOS along with their religious education. During the next two years the students will be tutored for Senior Secondary examination of NIOS along with their Madrasa teaching. Besides these students, in their senior classes, will also be taught about world religions and religious diversity of our country.

Urdu University: The Bridge

Maulana Azad National Urdu University Act, 1996 paved the way for the establishment of this university at Hyderabad in 1998. The mandate of the university is to promote vocational, technical and higher education through Urdu medium. This is an opportunity for Urdu-speaking people to enhance their education and skills through Urdu medium. It is a unique and only one of its kind in the country which has a dual mode of education, that is, regular as well as distance mode and has a National presence with campuses spread over many states of the country. It has all major streams of humanities, sciences, commerce, management, technology and education. When Dr Pavariz joined the University in 2015 as its Fourth Vice Chancellor, his first priority was to link it to madrasas. As per the norms of HRD Ministry, Madrasa graduates who pass out from those madrasas which are registered with State Madrasa Board are given equivalence according to the courses they have graduated in. But the courses which they are offered in Universities are confined to Arabic, Islamic Studies, Persian and Urdu. Hence their options remain limited even if they have studied some contemporary subjects like sciences or mathematics in these madrasas. Urdu University has devised two semesters 'Bridge Course' to facilitate lateral entry of these madrasa students into main-stream education. During these two semesters these madrasa pass outs are taught basics of the subjects they wish to opt for their degree course. Hence, University has prepared Bridge Courses for BSc, as well as BCom. They get direct admission to BA courses because of the subjects they studied at madrasa.

During their stay in MANUU they are imparted English communication skills to equip for further education or jobs. The university has a substantial number of madrasa students who are happily adapting to modern education. While many pursue masters in humanities, some of them even get into Urdu journalism, thereby providing the medium with a unique viewpoint, considering most journalists in English and Hindi media do not know much about Islam. This way Urdu University is a unique institution which is virtually acting as a bridge to connect madrasa students with modern education. Another notable feature of Urdu University is higher enrolment ratio of girl students. The university has 35 per cent girls in regular courses at its campuses and more than 60 per cent in distance mode. Most of these girls are from madrasas and from the weakest section of society. It also undertakes various training programmes for madrasa teachers and management to motivate them to adopt contemporary subjects. With government's focus on socio-economic educational empowerment of minorities especially girls, this university has potential to emerge as a hub of this transformation. With its experience of handling madrasa graduates, equipping them with various skills and training madrasa teachers in various subjects including teaching methodology, counselling and student psychology, it is capable to take up the task at the national level.

The Quran, Science and Our Madrasas

Today, Muslims across the world are divided on the basis of ethnicity, language, sect and so on, but, at the risk of a broad generalization, one can say that, by and large, they share a common feature: and that is, a distinct absence of the scientific spirit and low levels of scientific achievement and awareness. This is true, generally speaking, of Muslims across the world, especially in South Asia, which is home to the largest concentration of Muslims in the world.

The low level of interest in and awareness about science among Muslims generally is, in part, a result of their long-established educational system. Here the question arises: What sort of education and educational system are we talking about that is responsible for this malaise? If the fault lies with the secular education that is imparted in 'modern' schools, then, one can ask, why is it that people of other faiths who are also part of this educational system are advancing in science while Muslims are not? And if the fault lies in what is called the *deeni* or religious education that is imparted in madrasas, and if it be said that such education is inimical or indifferent to a scientific attitude, then, one can ask, how was it possible that for a long period, from the 7th to the 12th century, Muslim scientists who were products of this sort of education made great advances that laid the foundations of modern science?

There have been periods in human history when only religious learning was considered as education. People thought that through religious education they could acquire what the needed in order to be educated for their well-being. Here we should remember that knowledge has two sources: the first is revealed knowledge based on divine revelation. The second is the Book of Nature—the world around us, from which knowledge of nature can be drawn. In the beginning of human history, the only source of knowledge was divine revelation or *wahi Ilahi*. The teachings, including laws and rules, given by God were conveyed to humanity through prophets. This was then the only way for education and training. The Quran refers to this way of providing knowledge in several places.

As the human population increased and the social structure became more complex, God arranged for new ways and methods for people to acquire knowledge. Thanks to the efforts of many thinkers, over time new disciplines or sciences came into being and their scope expanded. It is widely recognized that for a long period till the 12th century Muslims were in the forefront of scientific scholarship, discoveries and inventions. In this era, many of the greatest philosophers, mathematicians, doctors and historians were Muslims. An important contribution of these early Muslim scholars was the experimental method, which is integral to modern science. The great interest in knowledge and research that emerged with the rise of Islam is a significant phenomenon. This thirst for knowledge among the early Muslims was produced by the Quran and by the encouragement given to knowledge by the Prophet Muhammad. Practising the teachings of the Quran, these Muslims became experts in many sciences and made significant advances in them, which was a major reason for the widespread Muslim influence that prevailed at this time over a large part of the world.

This continued till around the 12th century or so. But after this, Muslims slipped into the same sort of 'Dark Ages' that Europe slumbered in during the period of Muslim dominance, with the rise of superstition and anti-scientific attitudes. Increasingly, Muslims began treating knowledge of the world as useless. This was in sharp contrast to their attitude to science in their early history. It is something that even noted ulemma in India have also said more than once in the days gone by. For instance, well-respected Deobandi intellectual, Ashraf Ali Thanwi stated,

> It is, in fact, a source of great pride for the religious madrasas not to impart any secular education at all. For if this is done, the religious character of these madrasas would inevitably be grievously harmed. Some say that madrasas should teach their students additional subjects that would help them earn a livelihood, but this is not the aim of the madrasa at all. The madrasa is actually meant for those who have gone mad with their concern for the hereafter.

In contrast to this, an important aspect of the passion for knowledge among early Muslims was their holistic understanding of knowledge. Many of the top Muslim scientists of this time were not just experts in one or the other natural science but also in the religious sciences. Al-Kindi was a scholar of Islam and an expert in subjects like music and mathematics.

In a study of key scientists from the 7th to the 15th century, Charles Gillespie made a list of 132 people, of whom 105 were from the Muslim world. Many of the others who were from Europe had studied science in institutions in Muslim Spain. This means that around 90 per cent of the top scientists of this time were from the Muslim world. How things have changed since then! In a survey done in 1981, it was found that among the top 25 countries as far as publication of scientific literature annually is concerned, not one was Muslim! In 1996, less than 1 per cent of the authors of scientific articles published in journals across the world were Muslims! In the Middle Ages, when Muslims were around 15 per cent of the population of the world, they accounted, according to one estimate, for 90 per cent of scientific advancements. And today, when Muslims are around 22 per cent of the population of the world, their share in scientific writings is less than 1 per cent! That is one measure of the level and extent of Muslim decline.

There was a time when in Baghdad, on just one street there were some 200 bookshops, with books on subjects ranging from the Quran to astronomy, biology, mathematics and chemistry. People had personal libraries in their homes, and lovers of knowledge would organize literary sessions. The Quran was studied in the light of new discoveries and sciences. But today, leave alone Muslim bookshops or personal collections, it is difficult to find books by Razi or Jabir bin Hayyam or al-Kindi even in the libraries of Muslim educational institutions!

This story of Muslim decline in the field of scientific education is a dark chapter of human history. A community that made great contributions to science became a victim to blind imitation and hidebound traditionalism, because of which it fell behind in the field of science and technology. They stopped inventing useful things, and confined themselves to memorization of the sacred verses without understanding their meaning or the spirit behind them.

A principal factor that attracted many early Muslims to engage in research to study Nature was undoubtedly the Quran. At that time, the Quran was the Muslims' only focal point, and they were blessed by being in the company of the Prophet, from whom they received guidance. But after the demise of the Prophet, the situation began to change. This transformation happened slowly and in different ways. The Caliphate was replaced by authoritarian monarchy. Muslims began fighting among themselves. In this period, hadiths of the Prophet began being collected. Different views emerged regarding their status and authenticity and chains of transmission. Jurisprudential disputes and sectarian differences led to severe conflicts.

New lands came under Muslim rule, and while some people accepted Islam truly, some others did so for some worldly interest and to curry favour with the new rulers. At this time, some minds among the peoples whom the Muslims had vanquished reflected on the causes of Muslim dominance and thought of ways to put an end to it. It did not take them long to understand that it was the Quran—and only the Quran—that had united those who believed in it and in whose light of guidance they had become experts in many fields of knowledge and a powerful military, economic, social, political and civilizational force. These opponents of Islam also understood that it was impossible to make any changes in the Quran. So, they adopted a different method. In a very organized way, using different means, they sought to try to shift the Muslims' attention away from the Quran onto other things and to divert their thinking, concerns, efforts and abilities to other issues.

As a result of these conspiracies, the focus of a great many Muslims moved away from the Quran. The direction of their researches and investigation also accordingly shifted. Their understanding of Islam was diluted by literature other than the Quran. Texts began being written and popularized, some of which contained loopholes through which people sought to justify un-Islamic practices. New communities that entered the Muslim fold sought to introduce their own pre-Islamic practices under the garb of Islam, often using such non-Quranic texts as a means to seek to justify them. In this sense, 'Islam' became 'easy' for many people, who believed that they had earned a guarantee of admission to Paradise without having to abandon many of their ancestral customs and practices that were not sanctioned in the Quran. The character that the Islam of the Quran sought to produce was thus eclipsed.

Under the influence of these erroneous understandings of Islam that now emerged, many Muslims became/may have continued to recite and memorize the verses of the Quran but they became increasingly negligent towards the *ayat*s or signs of God that fill the Universe—the Book of Nature. The streams of knowledge dried up and an age of stagnation set in. The path of reason was shut and was replaced by the path of blind imitation. Increasingly, a notion, which had no sanction whatsoever in the Quran, became dominant that only certain subjects were 'religious' and were to be encouraged, while others were 'worldly' and hence to be shunned.

As Muslim political influence expanded, a significant number of Muslim rulers had patronized scientific learning. This had been another factor for many early Muslim scientists being attracted to engage in research. But when conflicts between Muslim rulers became endemic, this patronage began to decline.

Another factor that was responsible for Muslim intellectual decline at this time was that some Muslim rulers did not tolerate any criticism, not just of themselves but also of their religious beliefs. In such an atmosphere freedom of thought could hardly thrive. Continuous wars and oppression did not make for a conducive intellectual atmosphere. Monarchical autocracy became so opposed to Quranic teachings that righteous scholars or *ulema-e haq* were either compelled to oppose tyrannical rulers or else seclude themselves. As a result of these developments, the Islamic genius was almost completely eclipsed. The Muslim ulemma and other intellectuals were now entangled in metaphysics. No longer did the natural sciences and practical knowledge hold their interest. They revelled in heated debates that had no benefit for people—for both this world and for the Hereafter. They paid no attention to those sciences that could have enabled Muslims understand and benefit from the laws of Nature and help the cause of Islam.

Consequently, the Muslims' condition became just like the European Christians' had been during what was called their 'Dark Ages'. The latter had accepted Christianity in name, but it was only at a superficial 'spiritual' level and had no relation with 'worldly' welfare. They bore such hatred for 'worldly' knowledge that they declared the writings of Euclid and Plato to be false and burnt down libraries that preserved them.

Falling into the trap of the conspiracies of hypocrites, Muslims strayed far from the Quran. They divided knowledge into 'religious' (*dini*) and 'worldly' (*duniyavi*), a notion that has no sanction in the Quran. 'Worldly' sciences were declared as opposed to the *deen*. Given this narrowly restricted notion of worthy knowledge, centres of Muslim learning stagnated. This was accompanied by, and contributed to, Muslim economic, political and military decline. These two bodies of knowledge—'religious' and 'worldly'—were thought of as opposed to each other.

With the 'religious sciences' and the 'worldly sciences' being thought of as not just separate from each other but also as mutually opposed, it came to be believed that it was simply impossible for them to meet and mix. There was now a stark division in the ranks of Muslim intellectuals. Those whose only aim was to beautify the life of this world that lasts for only a few days focussed on what was called the 'worldly sciences', and those who wanted to beautify their Hereafter went in for what were now called the 'religious sciences'.

This notion of knowledge (*ilm*) still remains very widespread today. And our madrasas epitomize that. Today, Muslims remain saddled with the inheritance of the false notion of knowledge as being divided into two separate components—'religious' and 'worldly'. This reflects a widespread, but erroneous, understanding of the *deen* of Islam as a mere collection of some 'pillars', while in actual fact the *deen* is a complete way of life. However, is the sole purpose of knowledge to gather points for the Hereafter? Or is it to make this life better for ourselves, and those around us?

The division of knowledge that emerged later among Muslims, between 'religious' and 'worldly' knowledge, has also divided our educational institutions. Students of 'modern' schools do not get Islamic education, and in dini madrasas, students do not get comprehensive knowledge. Here the point needs to be considered that if children are not given a complete understanding of Islam, they cannot become beneficial people even if they excel in modern education. Knowledge and faith are two wheels of a vehicle. If even one is imbalanced, the vehicle will not work properly. What we need now is the sort of education based on the understanding of Islam as a complete way of life, as taught in the Quran. This would therefore reflect a holistic understanding of *ilm*, one that overcomes the rigid dualism that has characterized Muslim education for a long time. What needs to change is the belief that while donating money to mosques and madrasas is a means for continuous earning of merit (*sadqa-e jariya*), establishing institutions for 'worldly knowledge' is useless or at most an activity for worldly benefit and fame.

We need to train teachers who have a Quranic mentality and at the same time are experts in 'modern' subjects. We need 'model madrasas' where comprehensive education is imparted, where along with the translation and recitation of the Quran, students learn modern sciences and languages. These institutions could be based on the 10+2 model, and after finishing, students who wish to continue formal education could choose to study modern sciences in a college or a subject like Fiqh or Hadith in specialized madrasas. In this way, Muslim students would have a good knowledge of the teachings of the Quran and it can be hoped that their character and dealings will also be Muslim. The Quranic teachings would nurture their natural abilities of observation, experimentation, analysis, contemplation and research, abilities that are vital components of what is today called the scientific mentality. Scholars trained in this way will, one hopes, be able to present Islam in the correct and complete way.

Knowledge is the life of Islam,
and the pillar of faith

—PROPHET MUHAMMAD (PBUH)

Chapter 10

FUTURE PERFECT

At the height of Babri Masjid-Ramjanambhoomi struggle in the early 1990s, a young man went to a mosque-cum-madrasa in Delhi's Janakpuri colony to offer Friday prayers. Not accustomed to the ways of the city, he heard the azaan, and instinctively went in the direction of the call for prayers. Clad in jeans and T-shirt, the man started offering prayers with a bare head. Barely had the prayer concluded, however, that all hell broke loose. Men who had similarly gathered for the prayer, started shouting, screaming. While some went looking for buckets of water to clean the place, polluted by a man praying with a bare head, others looked for sticks to use on the errant first timer in the mosque-cum-madrasa compound. The main gate was shut to prevent the young man from slipping out. He had to be taught a lesson for polluting the sacred premises. However, the man was quick on his feet, and managed to slip out before other worshippers could harm him.

That was in the early 1990s. Cut to 2011. There is a similar mosque-cum-madrasa compound in Ghaziabad. A young man comes to offer his prayers at the crack of dawn. All worshippers stand in a neat row, shoulder to shoulder, ankle to ankle, to offer prayers. All but one, as it turns out. The young man, working in a call centre nearby, has not joined the congregation. Nobody objects. Nobody bothers. Most believe he would have got late for congregational prayers and hence is offering his own individual prayer. The same scene would repeat the next day. Then the next. It is only after that that the fellow worshippers noticed that the young man would come to the mosque-cum-madrasa but insist on saying his individual prayer rather than join others behind the imam, thus defeating the purpose of a congregational prayer.

Initially, he was advised by the elders, told about the benefits of praying in a group. 'The reward is 27 times for a group prayer in comparison to an individual prayer,' he was reminded. The patience though soon ran out. Tempers rose. Then the young man confided, insisting, 'I cannot pray behind this imam. He is not Barelvi. He is a Deobandi imam. I can only pray behind

Many madrasas and mosques continue to bar students and worshippers from other sects

Barelvis.' The argument soon petered out, but the young man's protest left a deep imprint. He stopped coming for prayers in future, the other worshippers went about their business as usual. The imam too resumed his leadership, but it left a question unanswered: What is it about madrasa education that divides the faithful? Why the madrasas that take pride in preparing hafiz students cannot simply stick to the message of the Quran and just be part of the ummah? Why should sectarianism be prevalent? But prevalent it is. For proof, one can see plenty of badly written, grammatically skewed but strong messages outside many places of worship in Rajasthan, Madhya Pradesh, Bihar and Maharashtra where a sect of Islam debars another from offering worship there. Some even threaten a monetary fine if an adherent of another sect were to enter! So much so, they would allow a non-Muslim to enter, but not a Muslim from another sect!

In some places, like the Janakpuri mosque, the reaction can be instant and violent, in others, it can be as instant but peaceful. For instance, at a large number of mosques in Bareilly, Ahmedabad, Islampur and Kishanganj, you cannot pray with a bare head or even recite the Quran without a skullcap. If somebody stands for prayer without covering his head, chances are, another worshipper would find for him a soiled, greasy plastic cap of garish green colour and put hit on his head in the middle of his prayer. At some mosques, if a man's ankles are not visible while he prays, or if he wears a half-sleeve shirt, he is given disapproving looks, and admonished at the end of the prayers. At others, if a man fails to symbolically kiss his fingers whenever the name of the Prophet is mentioned in azaan, he is considered as having gone astray. Almost everywhere, the length of a man's beard is the yardstick to measure piety! In most mosques, the imam is supposed to dress up in traditional kurta–pyjama, a pair of jeans, even if loose and comfortable, with a short-sleeve shirt is a no-no. Islam is reduced to the Orient! Since, many of the mosques are also used to impart Islamic instruction to children—many maktabs and madrasas operate out of masjids—it effectively means the ummah stands divided at the first step of learning. Indeed, madrasas are often guilty of one-upmanship, each trying to run down the madrasa of another sect. For years now, most madrasas have not only imparted teaching of only their sect to the pupils, they have also indoctrinated them against others. One is reminded of what a madrasa pass out, pursuing higher education at AMU, had to say about his madrasa days,

> In my madrasa many teachers forbid us from reading books and magazines published by other sects. English and Hindi newspapers were also banished. The languages were considered foreign to Muslims. Urdu was the only language allowed! In my case, it aroused curiosity, so I sneaked in books to be read against the torchlight at night or, even in the bathroom. In most others, it dulls it completely. So there is no window of opportunity to know about other sects. The students were punished if they were seen with literature from another sect, what to talk of non-religious books, magazines and newspapers, or books by non-Muslim authors. Once a scholar gave copies of the translation of the Quran by Maulana Wahiduddin Khan to all students. The authorities immediately confiscated them as Maulana Wahiduddin Khan is not regarded highly by them. He is, in fact, often regarded as a man who does the bidding of the Government. With this mindset, his scholarly works are ignored.

In fact, his experience was similar to a co-author of this book. When he decided to distribute copies of the translation of the meaning of the Quran, most mosques in Muslim-dominated areas of Delhi did not permit. And among those that did permit the distribution of the meaning of the Quran, there were volunteers of a Muslim jamaat that sought to physically stop the process.

It is this rigidity which closes the doors and windows to others, and gives rise to a situation where a man praying with a bare head is thought worthy of punishment, or a man refusing to stand behind an imam because he had studied at Deoband, and not a Barelvi madrasa. This leads to exclusion rather than encouraging the inclusion of all Muslims. At a time when the community is complaining of political exclusion, this silent exclusion within the community is helping none to foster bonds of brotherhood and togetherness. Instead of giving the community one platform to come together, it is confining each sect to a pigeonhole.

As a vast majority of Indian Muslims are Hanafis, it amounts to indoctrination with the Hanafi doctrine at most madrasas. The Hanafi madrasas fail to teach much about Shafi'i, Maliki or Hanbali sects. Same for Ahl-e-Hadiths. They do not teach about the Hanafis and the Deobandis. Almost all Sunni madrasas follow Dars-e-Nizami framed some 300 years ago. Very few modern-day additions have been made. Some Shia ones do the same too. But hardly any has space for Shia pattern of teaching with increasing emphasis on the so-called material subjects. It is vice-versa too. Frankly, the madrasas do not teach about Islam. They teach only one interpretation of Islam to youngsters. Thus in Deoband, it is the treatises of the Hanafi sect that gain prominent attention. There is hardly any space for other sects like Hanbalis, Malikis or Shafi'is. It is just assumed that a person will not need knowledge of these sects simply because they are in a small minority in India! Or that it is their interpretation of Islam is the only correct one, rest are all misguided!

The madrasas need to move beyond Ikhtilafiyat. No point running others down. It wears them down, drains their energy. And in the end, it is an exercise in futility. No madrasa or sect is either convinced or converted. It is best to follow what the Quran says through the last verse of Surah Kafirun: 'For you, is your religion, and for me is my religion.' To each, his own.

Incidentally, most of our madrasas since medieval India have spent a lot of time on fiqh. Back in Arabia it was understandable and desirable considering Islamic system prevailed. Even in medieval India it was understandable. The Muslims then were a small minority in the country. However, the kings were all Muslims. Often the religion of the kings was the religion of the kingdom. No king in medieval India is known to have ruled with shariah as the touchstone. Never mind they had lofty titles of being the Shadow of God on Earth and so on. Yet most of them did want the approval of the ulemma for their political and clearly un-Islamic even anti-Islamic actions. The ulemma, well groomed in Islamic law, were happy to oblige, often twisting the original teachings to suit the convenience of the ruler. Back then knowledge of fiqh gained state employment, something akin to modern civil services. The madrasas were like recruitment centres. Today, in a secular country run on the Constitution of India, the role of Islamic jurisprudence is reduced spectacularly to merely personal domain. It is reasonable to believe that if the sphere for a subject is reduced in society or polity, the time allocated for its teaching in the classrooms should be pruned too. It does not quite work out that way with our madrasas. Maybe the idea is to prepare the students for an unknown future when they would be able to implement what they assimilate now. However, in this crystal ball gazing it is important to remember to look beyond classical books of fiqh for they do not often deal with contemporary subjects. Their style, language and examples are caught in a time warp. They promote more enmity than debate and dialogue. They induce ennui rather than informed debate. Most commentaries taught to students are actually commentaries on commentaries! Certainly, not the ideal form for evoking interest. Worse, any fresh interpretation of the given text is often seen as an undesirable innovation, thus bet avoided. Shockingly, the ulemma who could not take a stand in consonance with the teachings of the Quran on the subject of instant triple talaq, arguing forcefully in favour of Talaq-e-Biddat, today consider a fresh interpretation as an invidious innovation!

In doing so, they forget that it is important to teach what the students can use in everyday life. One has to move on with time. For instance, today, it is imperative to teach youngsters about organ transplant and organ donation and their place in Islam rather than purifying water after a lizard falls into a well. It is crucial to teach young minds about the Creator but equally important to teach of His creations. It is worthwhile to remember verse 24 of surah Mohammad, 'Then do they not reflect upon the Quran, or are there locks upon (their) hearts?'

Yet the madrasas continue with their straitjacketed approach. As Waris Mazhari, editor of Tarjuman-e-Dar Ul 'Ulum is quoted by Sikand (*Bastions of the Believers*),

> Take the case of the Shara-i-Aqaid, a treatise on theology written some six hundred years ago. This book continues to be taught in many Indian madrasas, including Deoband. It is written in an archaic style, is full of references to antiquated Greek philosophy that students today can hardly comprehend.

The way madrasas teach, and the way they often cock a snook at each other points out to a system where the faithful have forgotten what is ilm or knowledge in the first place. Ilm, according to its dictionary meaning, stands for knowing something deservedly. Yet, our ulemma insist on separation of the religious form the secular! Or segregating the received or transmitted from the rational sciences! Why cannot they just let knowledge? It is the duty of madrasas to convey the true picture of knowledge in Islam. As centres of learning they cannot afford to submit to forces of obscurantism and negativity in the name of tradition. As Maulana Manazir Ahsan Gilani wrote in *Hindustan Mein Muslamanon Ka Nizam-e-Talim w Tarbiat*,

> I would like to ask is it a good thing that Muslims in the country and in the Islamic world are facing two types of education. Is it worthy to be kept as it is? Will it give any good result if the masses will be divided into two, one with the intellectuals and the other with the ulamma? This form of division and confrontation must be put to an end. Why the people did not sense the importance of the historical personalities who safeguarded the education from division for thirteen centuries? People don't realize it, but I consider the unity of the Muslims education system one of the great achievements. The entire thirteen centuries bear the witness that those who were called ulamma they were intellectuals and those who were intellectuals they were also called as ulamma. What a surprise! A single education system was

producing philosophers, mathematicians, doctors, engineers, muhaddis, mufassir, poets and Sufis.

Indeed, it is painful to see the education system divided into two. It is a consequence of our colonial masters' policy of divide and rule. The British, on the one side, allowed a category of people who were experts at Arabic and had memorized the Quran. On the other side, were those who were poets, doctors and engineers, etc. The former did not go to public schools and colleges, the latter did not go to maktabs and madrasas. With the decline of the Mughals, the avenues for state employment with knowledge of Persian, Arabic and Islamic jurisprudence came down drastically. With the rise of the British, the knowledge of English became a prerequisite for state employment. Consequently, more people gravitated towards public schools which almost assured them to at least a working knowledge of English, science and mathematics. In the absence of official support of the new state, madrasas were left to fend for themselves. With funds drying up, they were reduced to depending on charity for the institutions' sustenance. No longer were there Nawabs and kings ready to bestow acres of lands to madrasas. No longer were there imperial grants for the ulama. With the fortunes of the madrasas, the fortunes of the ulama declined too. As the institutions fell on bad times, and the clerics just managed to eke out a living, a thriving system of education that gave us composite learning fell into disuse. It was no longer the rich and the educated who sent their children to madrasas. The poor who had no means of education, and hardly enough to provide two meals to the family, started sending their children to Islamic seminaries. They asked no uneasy questions. They were content to memorize the Quran and learn about fiqh for some imaginary future. The little money they could earn as hafiz-e-Quran and the rise in social status that it brought, meant that both the students and their teachers slipped into a world where to take pride in the past is akin to be content with the present. Complacence and silence have replaced animated debates of the past. The madrasas need to demolish walls of sectarianism, overhaul their syllabus to survive with dignity. They need to change their teaching methodology in the age of smart classrooms and video conferences. The days of a blackboard, white chalk and physical punishment are long since over. It is an overhaul that will not bring them closer to an average school or trifle with their identity. It is a change that will make sure they survive into the next century. More importantly, they revive the days when astronomers and experts of Islamic jurisprudence, when mathematicians and experts of transmitted science stayed at the same place, studied at the same place. In cohesion, not exclusion can we hope for better days.

ABOUT THE AUTHORS

Ziya Us Salam is a noted literary and social commentator. A student of history from the University of Delhi, he is engaged in building bridges of commonality between communities through recourse to the Quran and the Vedas.

He has been associated with *The Hindu* for almost two decades and has been its Features Editor for North India editions for 16 years. At present, he is an Associate Editor, *Frontline*, and writes on sociocultural issues for the magazine besides doing book reviews.

A prolific and an acclaimed author, in 2019, he published *Lynch Files*, a take on victims of hate violence, and *365 Tales from Islam*, a book that aims to introduce Islam to children. In the previous year, he had released *Of Saffron Flags and Skull Caps*, a take on the challenges to the idea of India, and *Till Talaq Do Us Part*, a study of various divorce options available in Islam. His book *Delhi 4 Shows*, a study of cinemas since the talkie era began, was released in 2016. His book *Women in Masjid: A Quest for Justice* was released recently.

Ziya was a jury member of the International Film Festival of India (non-feature film, 2011), Best Writing on Cinema (2008) and Vatavaran.

M. Aslam Parvaiz, who holds a PhD in plant physiology, is currently the Vice Chancellor of Maulana Azad National Urdu University at Hyderabad, India. Earlier he was the Principal of Zakir Husain Delhi College (University of Delhi). He is a science communicator, founder and editor of *Urdu Science*, India's first and only popular science and environment monthly magazine published in Urdu since February 1994. He heads the Islamic Foundation for Science and Environment, a voluntary, non-profit, charitable organization.

He works on interface of Islam and science/environment. He interprets Quran from a scientific perspective and promotes holistic education. His contributed chapters are included in books/encyclopaedias published by reputed publishers. He has delivered invited lectures at Harvard, Yale, Toronto and many other institutions and organizations across the world.